D0857632

Phonological Markedness
and
Distinctive Features

Phonological Markedness
and
Distinctive Features

ARTHUR BRAKEL

INDIANA UNIVERSITY PRESS

Bloomington

The author acknowledges a generous publication subvention from the
Horace H. Rackham Graduate School of the University of Michigan.

*This book has been produced from camera-ready copy
provided by the author.*

Manufactured in the United States of America

Library of Congress Cataloging in Publication Data

Brakel, Arthur.
   Phonological markedness and distinctive features.

   1. Distinctive features (Linguistics) 2. Markedness
(Linguistics) 3. Semiotics. I. Title.
P218.B67 1983   414   82-49348
ISBN 0-253-34450-6
1 2 3 4 5 87 86 85 84 83

To Linda,
she has made it more worthwhile.

Contents

Preface

Phonological Markedness and Distinctive Features advances a set of articulatory primes, distinctive features, which differ from those in use among MIT or Jakobsonian phonologists as well as from those advocated over the last decade by Ladefoged (see Ladefoged, 1980). They are similar to Ladefoged's in that they are strictly articulatory, but they differ from all previously postulated sets of distinctive features because they are based on a set of *a priori* semiotic principles aimed at establishing the distinctive value (markedness) of a particular sound quality or articulatory gesture. I hope that my colleagues in phonology will recognize this set as both better phonetics and better phonology than any previous approach to the distinctive parameters used to distinguish the phonemes of human languages.

The exigencies of an academic career and teaching assignments in general linguistics, phonology, and the structures of Spanish and Portuguese have given me the task of conveying the knowledge of researchers such as Kenneth Pike, Charles Hockett, N. S. Trubetzkoy, Roman Jakobson, Morris Halle, Noam Chomsky, James Harris, Steven Anderson, J. C. Catford, Peter Ladefoged, and David Abercrombie to my students. In my teaching I have come to evaluate and modify their ideas and approaches as well as to adapt them to my own needs. This essay attempts to synthesize several different approaches to phonological description. It incorporates principles of phonemic analysis from American and Praguean structuralism, primarily their criteria for bestowing phonemic status on a particular segment in a particular system. It aims for the generality of generative phonology, and it seeks a phonetic accuracy similar to that advocated by Catford and Ladefoged. Beyond this, however, it suggests an interpretation of articulatory gestures and of sound systems but the interpretation is contained in the distinctive feature inventory itself.

Of course a work such as this would be unthinkable without the work of the researchers mentioned above and of many others not mentioned. In addition to the inspiration that I have received from the literature on phonetics and phonology, direct contact with scholars such as Lyle Campbell, Henning Andersen, Ronald Walton, Marianne Methuen, Steven Davis, and Rich Rhodes had helped me perservere at this task. I thank Ellen Kaisse, J. C. Catford, Ken Hill, John Goldsmith, and Ernst Pulgram both for the inspiration they have provided and for having read and criticized earlier versions of the manuscript. I am also extremely grateful to Pam Post who has twice shouldered the burden of typing it. I shall owe much of any felicity or success of this text to my critics and typist; however, I alone am responsible for its deviation from the norms of phonological description and I alone am responsible for whatever are its shortcomings. *Vale.*

Phonological Markedness
and
Distinctive Features

Chapter I
On the Phonetic Bases of Phonology

1.1.1 Many people reading the word "phonology" for the first time would probably guess that it was the name for the systematic study of sound in language. An appeal to a dictionary would quell any doubts: "The science of vocal sounds (= PHONETICS), esp. the sounds of a particular language; the study of pronunciation; *transf.* the system of sounds in a language." The professional linguist is not nearly as secure in defining this term, nor in delimiting the field known as phonology. Mattoso Câmara attests to this in his *Dicionário de Filologia e Gramática* (151) where he says "Phonology is a term used by different theoreticians in different and even contrary meanings." He lists three areas of study: the description of the sounds of a language; the value of the sounds in a given language; and the function of sounds in a given language.

1.1.2.1 Generative linguistics has not narrowed the definition of phonology. In recent years, linguists dealing with phenomena such as suballophonic variation, the articulatory peculiarities of individuals, segmental allophony, phonotactics, segmentation, neutralization of phonemic contrasts, morphophonology, supra-segmentals, and distinctive features all say that they work in phonology, all call themselves phonologists. Broadly speaking, phonology is that area of linguistic endeavor that deals with sound. This requires some clarification. An accepted way of looking at languages appears in the following model:

```
c
o
n               s
e  ───────────►  o
p   GRAMMAR      u
t  ◄───────────  n
s               d
```

This means that languages entail both sound and concepts. Sound is the principal medium through which human beings and cultures transmit concepts. The grammar of a language is the code that enables its speakers to translate systematic sound into concepts or concepts into sound. Thus, an extreme position would maintain that phonology and grammar are the same thing, that all grammar is involved in the translation of sound into concept and concept into sound.

1.1.2.2 The generative model of language (Extended Standard Theory) compartmentalizes grammatical phenomena as follows:

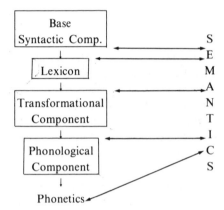

This model seems to suggest that phonology is a relatively superficial element of the grammars of languages; yet a quote from Chomsky (1965: 81) suggests deeper origins for phenomena which today we recognize to be phonological. He says "... let us review briefly the operation of the phonological component. ... Each lexical formative is represented by a *distinctive-feature matrix*..." That is, simply, that the phonetic parameters of phonology are located in the lexicon of universalist models of language. Morphology inevitably involves the use of phonological parameters; morphemes have phonetic substance. The model implies an interaction of sonorous and grammatical entities in the production of language. With generative grammar's claim of universality and its claim to be a model of the linguistic competence of the human race, it reflects the truism that human beings have minds that interpret the sound patterns of their languages, and that they have articulatory organs that produce sonorous representations of whatever they seek to express in language.

1.1.3 The insecurity of linguists in the 1970's concerning the definition of phonology can be witnessed in recent assertions of practicing phonologists. Foley, in *Foundations of Theoretical Phonology*, attacks the point of view I shall advocate. He says (52): "Only when phonology frees itself from phonetic reductionism will it attain scientific status." And (24) "As . . . the elements of psychological theory must be established without reduction to neurology or physiology, so too the elements of a phonological theory must be established . . . without reduction to . . . phonetic characteristics. . ." He derides all previous work in "phonology", maintaining (1) that his book ". . . presents . . . perhaps the only genuine theory of phonology in existence. . ." The bases of these assertions are dubious. Foley's abstract elements are nothing more than traditional articulatory phenomena that have been renamed with non-articulatory labels (cf. Brakel, 1980). In many cases articulatory data explain the phenomena more coherently than his abstract elements do. Kisseberth and Kenstowicz dedicate a major part (63–130) of their 1977 book to "The Non-Phonetic Basis of Phonology." They assert (63) that while "Phonological alternations generally have their ultimate source (historically speaking) in sounds being effected by the phonological context in which they occur . . . such contexts often become obscured through subsequent historical evolution. The phonetic basis of the original change may thus be lost, resulting in an alternation that . . . from a synchronic point of view lacks phonetic motivation." The authors examine phonemena such as rule inversions, telescoping, grammaticalization, and regularization (generalization) as linguistic phenomena that tend to obscure the articulatory motivation of certain morphophonemic sound changes in various languages. They also show that non-sonorous entities such as morpheme boundaries, grammatical categories, syntactic patterns, and the lexicality of certain items play an active part in the grammar of sound in a particular language.

1.1.4 No phonologist will deny any of Kenstowicz and Kisseberth's assertions. Many will maintain, however, that their particular brand of phonology does not concern itself with one or another phenomenon touched on by the former authors. Notwithstanding all that they say in *Topics in Phonological Theory*, the reason why their field of endeavor is still called phonology is that sound, in this case sound production or articulation, is inevitably involved in whatever phenomena they describe, in whatever rule they may write. It is wrong to consider non-sonorous entities and concepts as the base of phonology; they are theoretical constructs which linguists use to help systematize the sound that they know occurs in the production of all languages. Such constructs are ancillary, the base of phonology is sound produced in the human articulatory apparatus to be interpreted by the human brain.

1.2 To say that some phonological rules contain non-phonological abstract entities such as morpheme boundaries does not deny the articulatory base of phonology. Such a denial would necessarily conflict with the most obvious fact of language production—all human beings use virtually the same articulatory apparatus to produce the sounds of all languages. This articulatory tract, the organs of speech, is undeniably a linguistic universal. The specific interaction that articulation makes with the grammatical elements of a language is peculiar to whatever language the describer happens to be studying and depends upon the theoretical precepts and primes used. For example, a peculiarity of German and a few other central European languages is that all word-final stops are voiceless. We can express this fact discursively or we can write a rule for it. If we accepted the precepts of American structuralists: A. that the phoneme is the smallest unit of phonological analysis and B. the invariance principle—once a phoneme, always a phoneme; then we would have to consider all words which had a stem-final stop consonant which was voiced when an inflecting suffix was added, e.g. *bunde, bergen* but voiceless when no suffix was added *bund* [bunt] *berg* [berk] to have two allomorphs containing different phonemes. If we accepted the Prague school precepts concerning neutralization of contrasts, then we could represent the stems as /bunD/ and /berG/ and write rules governing the realizations of /D/ and /G/ according to their environments. Or finally, using distinctive features and the generative approach, a rule such as [+occlusion]→[+surd] ____# could be written and interpreted as either a phonotactic constraint of certain Germanic and Slavic languages or as a rule converting voiced stops to voiceless ones in word-final position; the language and data are the same, their interpretation differs according to linguistic schools.

1.3.1 In recent phonological work, linguists have represented articulation with distinctive features. Distinctive feature (hereafter, D.F.) inventories form an important cornerstone of the generative approach to phonology. If segments were the smallest phonological unit, unification of trans-segmental phenomena in a single rule would be cumbersome and, sometimes, impossible. The sub-segmental nature of the D.F. enables the rule writer to express phonological generalizations for an entire class of segments. For example, many languages have three nasal consonant phonemes /m, n, ñ,/ which contrast word initially, intervocalicaly, and utterance-finally but assimilate to the point of articulation of any consonant that follows a nasal. In a descriptive approach in which segments were the smallest unit, a rule to express such a generalization would look like this:

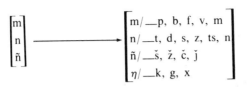

Using distinctive features the same rule appears as

$$[+\text{nasal}] \longrightarrow [\alpha\text{pt. of art.}] \Big/ \underline{\hspace{2cm}} \begin{bmatrix} +\text{contoid} \\ \alpha\text{pt. of art.} \end{bmatrix}$$

1.3.2 Beyond the notational advantages of using distinctive features in rules, a system, an inventory, of D.F.'s is a linguistic hypothesis concerning the phonetic parameters that are necessary to perform the task of describing the sonorous elements that human beings use to distinguish utterances. Any purportedly universal distinctive feature inventory says: 1) These and no more than these parameters are necessary to identify the distinctive articulatory possibilities of all human beings. 2) These parameters are adequate to write all the phonological rules of all human languages.[1] A distinctive feature inventory is the most abstract sonorous element in any grammar of sound, and at the same time it is the most concrete hypothesis about linguistic behavior. It is the focal point of the grammar of any language because it is essential for converting abstract concepts into concrete sounds and concrete sounds back into abstract concepts.

  1.3.3 Phonology is the sector of language study in which a hypothesis such as a D.F. inventory has a real chance of becoming a fact. Again, the universality of the articulatory tract is undeniable. The moving parts that produce all linguistic sounds are few, i.e., 4: the vocal bands, the velum, the tongue, and the lower lip; thence careful study of their operations in producing the sounds that linguists identify as segments should reveal precisely which gestures produce all the segmental contrasts of human languages. Some phonologists are embarrassed, however, about the status of the primes used to describe the distinctive sounds of speech. This embarrassment comes from the recognition that theories are explanations of phenomena wherein some of the facts are unknown. In phonology the facts of articulation are known, yet we have, to date, no widely accepted distillation of them into a system of primes (D.F.'s) which represents the distinctive articulations in the vocal tract.

1.3.4.1 Such a distillation is necessary because a satisfactory set of theoretical primes is essential to any investigation. The grammars that linguists create and the conclusions which they draw are shaped by the precepts and primes with which they operate. As examples let us examine two phonological descriptions made with different systems of primes. The contoids that are capable of closing a syllable in Portuguese are /r, l, n, z/. To describe them using the inventory of D.F.'s in Chomsky and Halle's *Sound Pattern of English* one needs the following rule:

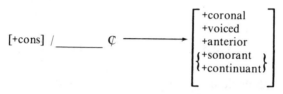

This is unsatisfactory because a disjunction is needed to include /n/ and /z/ in the same rule, thus no natural class emerges for this set of segments. The positive specifications suggest, to many linguists, that these consonants are highly marked. A description of them can be made using the system of D.F.'s to be proposed in the present study:

While the number of features is the same, there is no need for a disjunction; thus the consonants pertain to a phonetic natural class. The negative specifications suggest, as well, that these contoids are much less contoidal than others, that they are the unmarked members of the fricative, nasal, lateral, and "vibrant" series of Portuguese phonemes.

1.3.4.2 Another phenomenon which can be described more efficiently with different tools of analysis is what is generally agreed to be contoidal weakening in Spanish and Iberian Portuguese. Intervocalic /b, d, g/[2] are realized as approximants. To represent this in SPE features the following rule is necessary:

The addition of a feature, [+continuant], to many linguists suggests the addition of a mark which is the opposite of a weakening. In the Chomsky-Halle school of phonology, rules such as this necessitated an elaborate marking mechanism which maintains that certain features represent markedness in certain environments and non-markedness in others. In the system to be advocated here, the following rule describes the intervocalic weakening of voiced stops:

$$\begin{bmatrix} -\text{surd} \\ +\text{occlusion} \end{bmatrix} \longrightarrow [-\text{occlusion}]/\ \ \text{V} \underline{\quad\quad} \text{V}$$

Besides needing fewer features to describe the phenomenon, contoidal weakening is symbolized by the loss of a phonological prime.

1.3.5 Two rules are hardly sufficient for the justification of a new theory of phonology. I shall endeavor to show in Chapter III, where I justify my revision of the inventory, that the features I propose have greater observational, descriptive, and explanatory adequacy than those suggested by Chomsky and Halle (1968) (hereafter SPE). I shall also contrast my D.F.'s with the acoustic primes of Jakobson, Fant, and Halle (1952) in Chapter IV.

1.3.6 Another advantage of theoretical work in phonology and D.F.'s lies in the comparability of hypotheses. Because of the finite articulatory base that human beings have and use to create sound systems, the phonological primes that linguists propose are finite and, as theories, the best D.F. inventories are the simplest ones. The Chomsky-Halle inventory of D.F.'s contained 25 segmental primes of interest here, which, if they could combine freely, would specify a total of 33,554,432 segments (2^{25})—certainly many more than linguists have any need to identify. Obviously, the total number they can specify, because of the physical limitations of the vocal tract, is somewhat less than the above figure, but I doubt that even .01% of the power of this theory is necessary to identify all the segments that linguists have needed to describe in the entire history of linguistics. The Jakobson, Fant, and Halle (1952) (hereafter, JFH) D.F. inventory (defended again in Jakobson and Waugh, 1979 hereafter J&W) contains 12 primes, but, to function, will need two more (see Chapter IV) which will give it a total of 14 primes and a generative capacity of 2^{14} or

16,384 segments. These D.F.'s do not include prosodic considerations such as length nor air stream features. Including these in the inventory I propose, gives a total of 19 features and a generative capacity of 2^{19} or 524,288 segments which is 1.56% as strong as the SPE inventory.

1.3.7.1 While this work and much of the linguistic research of the 1970's would be meaningless or impossible without Chomsky and Halle's SPE, their book has been criticized on many grounds: its D.F. inventory, its approach to markedness, and even, the observational descriptive, and explanatory adequacy of the whole system as a theory of phonology. Ladefoged (1971) argues that some of the SPE D.F.'s are descriptively inadequate and that their strict binarity does not prevail at the level of surface phonetics. Lisker and Abrahamson (1971) criticize Chomsky and Halle's features which purport to account for laryngeal control during the production of sound as well as their claim that the features proposed in SPE represent articulatory reality. Campbell (1974) shows the inadequacies of SPE D.F.'s in their specification of natural classes of segments. Lass (1976: 168–212) maintains that the SPE D.F.'s are often unable to make generalizations and unite natural classes in individual languages. Kuipers (1975) attacks SPE on the grounds that the semiotic foundation on which the phonetic framework and the marking theory were built was less than solid. Foley (1977) claims that SPE and generative phonologists in general have not achieved any satisfactory explanations of phonological phenomena.

1.3.7.2 Certainly these attacks come as no surprise to Chomsky and Halle—they anticipated them before elaborating their primes (298): "We are well aware of the many gaps in our knowledge that make the success of this undertaking somewhat problematical ..." In view of this, the unquestioning support that their original postulates have been given (e.g. Mira Mateus, 1975; Anderson, 1976) is surprising. Chapter 9 of SPE begins with the caveat (400):

> The entire discussion of phonology in this book suffers from a funda-
> mental theoretical inadequacy ... There is nothing in our account of
> linguistic theory to indicate that the result would be the description of a
> system that violates certain principles governing human languages ...
> we have failed to formulate the principles of linguistic theory, of
> universal grammar, ... we have not made any use of the fact that the
> features have intrinsic content.

1.4 I shall show that several of the features really have no intrinsic content (vocalic, syllabic, sonorant), and that the implied content of some is actually counter-productive to efficient description of sound systems. I shall attempt to reduce the generative power of the D.F.

inventory by reducing the number of primes, yet I shall increase its observational, descriptive, and explanatory adequacy.

Footnotes

[1]Phonological rules represent actual articulatory gestures of speech sounds according to their systematic, potentially distinctive, properties. Any detailed, phonetically accurate descriptions or denotations of actual articulations in particular languages usually involves minutia that are phonologically redundant or unimportant in distinguishing utterances' meanings.

[2]In Portuguese, the best analysis of these sounds is that they are occlusives. They are obligatorily so only after a homorganic nasal or lateral. It is, however, never wrong to pronounce them as occlusives. The point of the discussion on this matter is, simply, that the SPE features do not portray their allophony in a satisfactory manner.

Chapter II
Semiotic Foundations for
Distinctive Features

2.1 Chomsky and Halle ended *Sound Pattern of English* with a chapter titled Epilogue and Prologue: the Intrinsic Content of Features. This chapter contains a mechanism designed to accommodate the primes they proposed to general facts of phonology and to the authors' notions of naturalness. The primes Chomsky and Halle postulated forced them to propose conditions for marked and unmarked values: positive specifications were considered marked in certain environments and unmarked in others, just as negative specifications were marked values in some environments and unmarked in others. For example, positive specifications for [voice] or [continuant] were unmarked intervocalically because the mechanics of sound production, articulation, seemed to favor them there. Rather than append a mechanism for adjusting my theoretical primes to the reality of language, I shall establish a semiotic theory first, then use this theory to elaborate an inventory of distinctive features.

2.2 An *a priori* system of language semiotics should begin with a definition of language. For the purposes of this study, a language is a systematic historical-cultural institution of communication developed by human beings over the ages to unify, divide, stratify, and occupy one another. Vocal language potentiates communication through the use of acoustically discernable, systematic modifications of and impediments to the flow of air between lungs, lips, and nostrils. These modifications and impediments produce sounds which are transmitted through the air and apprehended by the human ear and interpreted by the human brain. The gestures which produce these sounds are overlays on the non-communicative activities of the articulatory tract, breathing and eating. Breathing and eating are non-communicative acts and differ from linguistic acts because the noises they produce:

10

coughs, wheezes, smacks, belches, etc., although meaningful, especially when they are voluntary, are symbolic and analogic rather than semiotic and digital. To communicate with language human beings produce temporal artifacts in the form of semi-arbitrary articulatory gestures which in turn create other artifacts—sound wave configuations or systematic silence. As part of their enculturation, human beings, as senders and receivers of messages, learn the code that interprets the systematic production or suspension of sounds in their language, and they learn to associate meanings with the sound patterns of their language.

2.3 The first act of human sonorous communication is infantile crying, the undisciplined production of laryngeal resonance. Crying is a psycho-motor response to basic needs, among these are air and food. Infants learn its efficacy very early because their guardians attend to their needs as a response to their crying. As infants are enculturated, this laryngeal resonance and the unconstrained babble of early infancy are molded into the sound system used in the infant's culture. This sound system, a cultural product, can be analyzed into D.F.'s which represent either the sound spectra (acoustic data) or the articulatory gestures used to create the sounds. On both a physiological and a semiotic level, distinctive features are accretions, structures super-imposed on the basic act of communication, laryngeal resonance, i.e. crying. An articulatory D.F. inventory is a registry of the gross gestures necessary for sonorous communication, a registry of the marks that human beings make on the air stream.

2.4.1 The concept of markedness has intrigued and frustrated scholars since it first appeared in the writings of the Prague School linguists. Baltaxe (1978: 35–47) traces its history and interpretation from the writings of theoreticians who coined the term, up to the works of contemporary linguists. She asserts that ". . . the concept of markedness, as it exists in its current form . . . should be taken as a proposal that awaits a great deal of further thought and exploration." Kuipers (1975) refers his readers to Jakobson (1968) for what he feels to be the proper approach to markedness, an approach in which (SPE, 404) ". . . the marked coefficient of a feature was assumed to be + and the unmarked coefficient always –." A theory of marking in which the marked coefficient is always + is a much simpler (i.e. stronger) theory than the one which allows the conditions and adjustments that Chomsky-Halle proposed. The strong approach should be examined closely to see if it works effectively in, at least, the paradigmatic specification of phonological systems.

2.4.2 Kuipers categorically rejects Chomsky and Halle's proposals on markedness and optimistically asserts (Kuipers, 43) that

As to phonological markedness, here, too, a simple approach is ...
enlightening ... If we write in black on a white background the black
'stands out' and is 'marked.' That of which there is less, that which is less
usual, will be experienced as 'marked' ... therefore, that one of a
correlated pair of phonemes which occurs more often, will tend to
become the 'background' against which its correlate stands out.

2.4.3.1 Notwithstanding this optimism, it is not easy to find an
articulate formulation of a theory or program for markedness in any
school of linguistic description. The closest approximation to a
satisfactory program of marking appears in Greenberg's (1966) *Language Universals with Special Reference to Feature Hierarchies.*[1] He
accepts the idea that a mark is a positive something and suggests the
following 5 principles for approaching markedness (13–24 and 58–59).
1) The feature which occurs in neutralization is unmarked. When in a
particular class of environments no contrast occurs within a set of
lexemes or phonemes which differ from each other only in a single
feature, it is the unmarked feature which appears in this environment.
2) The unmarked member of a pair of phonemes is more frequent in
texts. 3) Unmarked members have greater allophonic variety than
marked members. 4) The number of phonemes with the marked
feature in the phonemic inventory of a given language is always smaller
than or equal to the number with the unmarked feature. 5) The basic
allophone, defined in terms of phonologic independence from its
environment, is the unmarked one.

2.4.3.2 Principles 2 and 4 are capital to the semiotic foundations of
the distinctive feature inventory I shall propose. Principle 3 will have
to be substantiated in interlinguistic studies once a satisfactory set of
phonological primes has been derived. It seems, however, that it is
correct; least marked segments will have relatively few positive specifications, thus they should have greater phonetic flexibility than highly
marked members of the same system, provided that there is ample
phonological space around the unmarked segment. For example:
according to this principle and the system of D.F.'s that I propose, the
least marked contoidal phoneme in Portuguese is /r/, the most highly
marked, /š/. Using the system of primes that I propose in this study
they are specified as follows:

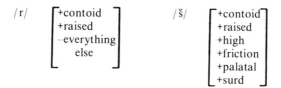

/r/ ⎡ +contoid   ⎤   /š/ ⎡ +contoid ⎤
     ⎢ +raised   ⎥   ⎢ +raised ⎥
     ⎢ −everything   ⎥   ⎢ +high   ⎥
     ⎢   else   ⎥   ⎢ +friction⎥
     ⎣   ⎦   ⎢ +palatal ⎥
                                   ⎣ +surd   ⎦

/š/ has, in standard dialects of Portuguese, no significant allophonic variation; and it occurs only syllable initially;[2] /r/, on the other hand, occurs in the following environments: C__V, V__V, V__C, __#. When it occurs in syllable initial consonant clusters, it often assimilates in voice to the preceding consonant. When syllable final it may have, in Carioca Portuguese, any of the following realizations: [x, g, h, r, ɹ, Ø, x̃, g̃]. This happens partially because of the few intrinsic positive specifications of the phoneme and because none of these sounds represents any phoneme other than /r̃/, which contrasts with /r/ only intervocalically. I am, however, somewhat ill-at-ease with Principle 3. The allophonic variation of a set of segments seems to be language-specific rather than phonetically predetermined by a set of abstract principles. In American English, the voiced stops have virtually no allophonic variation whereas the voiceless ones may be aspirated, flapped,[3] glottalized, or articulated with no aspiration. On the other hand, in Portuguese and Spanish, voiceless stops have no significant allophonic variation whereas the voiced stops do. Linguists need to understand the dynamics of phonological systems much better before Principle 3 can be an axiom of phonological markedness.

    2.4.3.3 Principle 5 is taken for granted in D.F. approaches to phonemic inventories. Segments are specified to the point that is necessary to distinguish them from their closest coordinates, provided that they are distinguished from all segments. If a particular allophone of a phoneme acquires extra features, i.e. is phonetically more complex than the basic allophone, the redundant features are added in a phonological rule. For example, the voiceless stops of English contrast with all other segments in that language by virtue of their being [+occlusive +surd]. Their aspirated allophones are phonetically more complex than the basic phoneme, but this complexity is not necessary to distinguish them from the other phonemes of English. The aspiration of these consonants is mandatory in certain environments and must be reflected in a rule in the phonological grammar of English, and this rule adds a feature to their specification.

    2.4.3.4.1 Principle 1 has its basis in dicta of the Prague School. Trubetzkoy (*Introduction to the Principles of Phonological Descriptions*, 27–28) maintained:

> Two phonemes or, as the case may be, phonemic classes between which a neutralizable contract exists, are said to be especially closely related to one another, and, when this neutralizable contrast is one which can be described as presence or absence of a particular feature, the phonemes in question are termed respectively the 'marked' form and the 'unmarked' form. The unmarked form here is always that phoneme which, where the contrast in question has been neutralized, appears as the sole representa-

tive of the relevant pair of phonemes—provided, of course, that the situation is not obscured by assimilation ... For determining the phonological content of the individual phonemes and for the understanding of the whole structure of the relevant system ... any phonological description ... must be written in such a way as to reveal just which phonological contrasts are neutralizable in the language under study and which terms in such contrasts are to be regarded as marked, or, as the case may be, unmarked.

It is remarkable that this principle still is accorded currency today. The statement has led to confusion in the writing of many linguists, including Greenberg. Neither Greenberg nor Trubetzkoy give us any reason why the unmarked phoneme occurs in a position of neutralization. In the Portuguese data, for example, /r/ and /r̃/ contrast only intervocalically: *caro* 'dear' *carro* 'car.' There are environments where only /r̃/ occurs: #___, n___, z___, l___; where only /r/ appears: p___, t___, k___, (see above); and there are environments where the phoneme /r/ occurs exclusive of /r̃/: ___#, ___¢. In the last of these three environments, prestige dialects of Brazilian Portuguese realize /r/ regularly as [x], the normal realization of /r̃/, yet morphophonemically is it /r/. The phrase '... obscured by assimilation ...' is of supreme importance. While it is difficult but not impossible to make a case for the assimilatory nature of much of the allophony of /r/ in Portuguese, many neutralizations of phonemic contrasts are the result of assimilation of one kind or another. Common examples are: 1) regressive assimilation of point of articulation of nasal consonants contiguous to other consonants in Spanish, Portuguese, and Italian; 2) regressive or progressive assimilation of voice between contiguous consonants; 3) vowel harmony.

2.4.3.4.2 The neuturalization of intervocalic /t/ and /d/ in North American English can be seen as assimilation. With the loss of this contrast in words like *latter* and *ladder* the /t/ loses its [surd] quality and becomes assimilated to its environment as far as its voicing is concerned.

2.4.3.4.3 The neutralization that researchers refer to most often when dealing with markedness is that which occurs in Germanic and Slavic where intervocalic voiced consonants alternate with surds word finally: Polish [šfábe] 'Krauts', [šfáp] 'Kraut'. Here again, a case can be made for considering the devoicing of the word final stop as an assimilation—an assimilation to the voicelessness of a potential pause which may occur after any word. But linguists have concluded from data similar to the example above that stop consonants are naturally voiceless, that voiced stops are marked because air is impeded at the point of articulation yet the vocal bands continue to vibrate to produce

voiced stops. Because of his adoption of this tenet, Greenberg is forced
to acquiesce to a position on the markedness of segments which
foreshadows Chomsky and Halle's (24):

> It should be noted that in some cases we had what might be called
> conditional categories for marked and unmarked. For example, whereas
> for obstruents, voicing seems clearly the marked characteristic, for
> sonants the unvoiced feature has many of the qualities of a marked
> category.

In this work I shall challenge this assertion and adopt the feature [surd]
(i.e., voicelessness). Thus voiceless segments, be they stops, fricatives,
laterals, nasals, or vocoids are marked. That is, [−surd] phonemes will
normally exceed the number of [+surd] phonemes in text segmental
frequency counts, and, normally, the [−surd] member of a pair will be
more proponderous than the [+surd] member.

2.4.4.0 Incorporating Principles 2, 4, and 5 from Greenberg; considering 3 as moot, and rejecting 1 as baseless, I shall proceed to
discuss six other parameters of markedness that Greenberg touches on
in his treatise. The following parameters are interrelated facets of
markedness: exclusion, complication, irregularity, infrequency, impli-
cation, and accumulation.

2.4.4.1 A form or category which excludes the other members of a
set to which it belongs is the marked category and its markedness
should be specified positively. In languages which have grammatical
gender, as the Romance languages do, [feminine] is the marked
category because its use excludes many members and identifies a
culturally determined perceptual minority. On the other hand, the non-
feminine (traditionally called the "masculine") gender is the unmarked
category. When we say in Portuguese *Tenho 16 filhos, 15 moças e um
rapaz*, "I have 16 children, 15 girls and one boy" we use the unmarked
form for "offspring" because we can include the marked category
[feminine] as a subset. On the other hand, were we to say *Tenho 16
filhas* "I have 16 daughters" we preclude any possibility of there being a
son among those 16 offspring. Traditional distinctive features also
perform this function: [+nasal] or [+lateral] identify minority subsets in
the totality of segments in any phonemic inventory. Negative specifications such as [−nasal] or [−lateral] will characterize majorities. In other
words, there will always be more segments not marked for a given
feature than segments so marked.[4]

2.4.4.2 A form which is more complex in the number of elements
that comprise it usually is the marked category since it designates a
subset of the set in which it is included. In the Hebrew utterance / ha

izraelí tov/ "The Israeli is a good person" the morpheme –*i* represents all citizens of Israel. On the other hand, if we say / ha izraelít tová/ 'the Israeli woman is good' we make no linguistic judgment about the other half of the population because we have used the marked forms and refer to only the perceived minority. The tenses and aspects of Romance languages illustrate this as well: if we say in Spanish *Damos dinero a los pobres* 'We give money to the poor', such an utterance can be used to designate 1) habitual action *Todas las navidades damos dinero a los pobres*, 'Every Christmas we . . .'; 2) futurity *Hoy es sábado, damos dinero a los pobres mañana* 'Today is Saturday, we('ll) give . . . tomorrow'; 3) historical present (e.i., timeless) *Nos levantamos a las siete, vamos a misa a las ocho, damos dinero a los pobres, y finalmente almorzamos* 'We get up at 7, go to mass at 8, give alms to the poor, and finally, we eat.' 4) Hypothetical action *Si damos dinero a los pobres nos sentimos felices* 'If we give . . . we feel happy'. In contrast, the morphologically complex, albeit portmanteau and highly irregular, form *dimos* 'we gave [perfective]' can be used only to indicate past action at a certain point without future, present, or hypothetical implications. Complexity in phonology is reflected by the accumulation of marks to specify a given segment: a^5 is universally accepted as a simple sound in human articulation. The organs of speech are at rest with the larnyx vibrating. A sound such as *ü* (agreed to be more marked than *a*) is much more complex since its articulation involves the raising of the tongue blade and the rounding of the lips—additions or marks on the egressive air stream. This complexity is paralleled by *ü*'s relative infrequency as a systematic sound in the languages of the world and its low frequency relative to other vowels, in languages where it has phonemic status.

2.4.4.3 Irregular or non-general members of a particular set are marked members of whatever set they pertain to. Grammatical gender again serves to illustrate this point. In Portuguese most feminine (marked) entities are designated by the use of the feminine gender suffix, –*a*.

Gloss	Non Feminine	Only Feminine
owner	dono	dona
sibling	irmão	irmã
young person	moço	moça
spouse	esposo	esposa

MARKED MEMBERS

parent	pai	mãe
horse	cavalo	égua
spouse of offspring	genro	nora

The marked members are learned by rote rather than rule. In phonology, sounds that do not use the egressive pulmonic air stream are exceptions to the general rule that egressive pulmonic air is the principal source of sound systems, thus glottalic and velaric air stream sounds receive special marking for their special status.

2.4.4.4 Infrequency or rarity is another trait of marked forms. Greenberg showed (43) that singular items outnumber plurals and that cardinal numbers occur more than ordinal numbers in text frequency counts. Articulatorily simple sounds are more frequent than complex ones: *a* likely outnumbers all other segments in overall frequency both intra- and inter- lingually; a sound like *a* occurs in all languages, one like ë in relatively few.

2.4.4.5 A mark implies the existence of its negation. That is, a feature such as [+nasal] is only invoked when nasal sounds contrast with non-nasal sounds in a given language. The existence of a first and second person in a grammar implies, through the negation of both, the existence of an unmarked (third) grammatical person.

2.4.4.6.0 The accumulative facet of markedness applies both to segments and to systems. As a segment becomes more and more complex, its complexity is reflected in more and more positive specifications. As a system becomes more complex, more and more primes are necessary to distinguish all the items in it. We may therefore refer to systems as more or less marked according to the number of items and rules needed to describe them. The feature acquisitional hierarchy that Jakobson proposed in *Child Language, Aphasia, and Phonological Universals* implies a successive acquisition of greater and greater markedness in phonological systems, but late acquisitions in the segmental inventory are not necessarily highly marked. For example, *l* and *r* can be shown to be simple and unmarked relative to *p*'s and *k*'s, yet their existence implies the presence of more complicated segments.

2.4.4.6.1 Jakobson maintains that the acquisition and decay of phonological systems operate as mirror images of one another: the last segments acquired are the first to be lost, the earliest acquisitions, the last to be lost. An examination of his ontogenesis, because of its putative universality, will be part of the formulation of a theory of phonological markedness since we shall see how the addition of distinctive marks conforms to the principles of markedness independently set up here.

2.4.4.6.2 The contrast between contoid and vocoid is held to be universal. It is the first to appear in a child's phonology and is the last to disappear in speech pathology. The first vocoid is a sound like *a*, the first contoid, a sound like *p*. At this point, all the sounds are either [±contoid] with the positive specification indicating the later acquisition.[6] The next contoid to appear is *m* [+nasal] after which *t* [+raised] appears. According to Jakobson (48) these are the minimal ingredients for any phonological system. Vocoidal differentiation proceeds from *a* to *i* [+high], then to either *u* or *e* which produces either triangular *i~a~u* or linear *i~e~a* systems and the minimal number of primes for vowel systems [±raised].

2.4.4.6.3 While Jakobson does not point it out, the development of a minimally differentiated vowel system, which occurs after the minimally differentiated consonant system has developed, pushes the consonant system towards further development with the addition of either [high] or [dorsal] to the acquirer's repertoire. Now, a stop such as *k* [+high +dorsal] can appear. After the acquisition of a *k*, fricatives appear with an *s* as the basic segment (55). Jakobson is not explicit about the rest of the ontogenesis. He maintains that for any affricate to appear, the system must already contain the homorganic fricative. Once friction is added to segmental inventories, consonants contrast in two primes: [nasal] and [friction]. For [occlusion] to become a distinctive feature, a contoid must appear that is either an affricate or an *r*. Affricates are both fricative and occlusive, *r*'s are neither. Sounds such as *r* and *l* emerge late in the acquisition schedule, but are the first to be affected in the decay of phonological systems, either through linguistic change involving simplification or through the speech pathology of an individual. After these consonants have been added to repertoires, there may be even further elaboration—the acquisition of tenseness, labiality, and nasality in the vocalic sector, for example.

2.4.4.6.4 If Jakobson is correct, phonological systems seem to develop in a dialectic process—going from diametrical oppositions towards successive approximations. The maximal contrast, *a~p*, involves complete opening vs. complete closure at the outermost point of the vocal tract. Nasality is a synthesis: *m* consists of the oral closure of *p* along with the voicing and constant, albeit rerouted, flow of the egressive air of *a*. The addition of *t* [raised] adds a new parameter and is another diametrically opposed expansion because place of articulation or use of tongue has become distinctive in contoidal articulation. This new parameter is put to use in the vocoid inventory: the addition of an *i* makes tongue position a distinctive category in the vocalic subset of segments. Once *e* or *u* is added, either relative tongue height or backness becomes distinctive. The addition of the parameter [high] suggests a synthesis of articulatory properties present since [high] approaches contoidal articulation; the addition of [dorsal] suggests a diametric opposition since articulation in a different part of the mouth has become distinctive.

2.4.4.6.5 The last segments to appear in contoidal inventories, *r* and *l*, are, at least aerodynamically, negations of contoidal properties. They are the most vocoidal of the contoids. Conversely, late acquisitions in vocoidal inventories, front rounded vowels, and nasal vowels, have more and more marks, thus are more akin to contoids. Contoids and vocoids begin as polar opposites and gradually approach one another as phonological systems become more and more elaborate.

2.5 What should we ask of a D.F. inventory as a theory of phonological systems? A theory of phonological systems should, in a manner as economical as possible, 1) be able to specify all of the contrasting segments that linguists have found or are likely to find in the languages of the world; 2) be able to describe all of the articulatory changes of distinctive consequence that occur in human speech sounds as defined by the inventory, 3) be able to explain sound changes in a manner consistent with what is known about the mechanics of the articulatory tract, 4) provide a positive mark for each distinctive sound segment type that linguists describe; 5) describe complex sound with more positive specifications than those necessary for simple sounds; 6) reflect unusual or unexpected articulatory gestures and air stream initiators with positive specifications, since these are considered marked; 7) reflect the frequency of common sounds with fewer positive specifications; 8) reflect the greater complexity of phonological systems with a larger number of distinctive parameters specifying the segments; 9) imply the presence of other articulatory gestures which are not marked; 10) establish a neutral segment in the description of each phonological system (This neutral segment should be the *a* like sound, the segment with no positive specifications. It will be the semiotic backdrop for all the other sounds of the language and all other sounds will be marked in relation to it. This is, of course, not to imply that the *a*'s of any two languages are phonetically the same, rather that all languages have a backdrop phoneme.); 11) contain no feature which is necessary for the specification of segments in all phonological systems. According to the principles established in this chapter, anything that is universal in language cannot be a mark since that which is universal serves as a backdrop for further modification. For example, [voice] cannot be a mark because all languages have voiced segments. On the other hand, the converse of voice, [surd], is a mark because it implies its converse, there must be voiced sounds for voiceless ones to function; there are languages which contain no voiceless phonemes, and there are languages in which the voicelessness of segments can be shown to be redundant.[7] A mark is non-universal. By adhering to these principles, a D.F. inventory is a theory of phonological markedness.

2.6. I would like to express caution concerning the implications to be drawn from the apparently diametrical expansion of distinctive feature inventories (phonological systems). While many scholars appear to claim that binarity is intrinsic to the way all human beings think, such a conclusion may be premature. The binary analysis of speech sounds predisposes us to see the development of segmental inventories as diametrical. While the binary approach facilitated alphabetic writing, it is not the only way to study phenomena, and it is not a particularly strong hypothesis about language or human behavior, if we can continue to add binary parameters in order to distinguish or specify all the data we apprehend. (I refer the reader back to the power of the Chomsky-Halle D.F. inventory). I claim no psychological reality for the features I propose. They are analytic tools tailored to the mechanics of the articulatory tract and the principles outlined in this chapter.

Footnotes

[1] Even though *Language Universals* preceded *SPE* by two years the authors of *SPE* did not acknowledge Greenberg's work on markedness.

[2] The best analysis of syllable final sibilants in Portuguese considers them to be allophones of /z/, realizable as [s, z, š, ž] according to dialect and position (Brakel, 1977: 139-140).

[3] Some speakers of English flap intervocalic /d/ 's: *bed* [béd] *bedding* [bédIŋ]. This does not occur in my speech. Intervocalic /t/ and /d/ are realized as [d]. The point that the voiceless stops of English have a wider range of allophonic variation than the voiced stops is incontrovertible.

[4] A possible exception to this generalization is the major class feature [contoid]. Phonological systems regularly contain more consonants than vowels, although when all segments of a relatively large text are counted, vowels and consonants occur in equal numbers—roughly 50% of the corpus will be vowels even thought the vowel phonemes number much less than the consonants, Brakel (1979a), Alarcos LLorach, (1968: 198-200).

[5] When referring to a segment with no regard to the linguistic sytem in which it occurs, I italicize. The segment *a* is a low, central, unrounded, non-nasal, tense, vocoid.

[6] Other features of a contoid sound such as *p* are redundant at this point. Its voicelessness, labiality, and occlusion play no role. Admittedly, any one of these features could be considered to be the first acquired.

[7] Voicelessness does not play a distinctive role in the phonological systems of Andoa, Gadsup, and Nunggubuyu. Voiceless phonemes do not occur in Dyribal. See Appendix A.

Chapter III
Distinctive Features Revisited: Towards a Stronger Theory of Phonology

3.0.1 A D.F. inventory is a hypothesis about all the phonological systems in the world. It says that these and no more than these features are necessary to characterize all the phonological systems produced by the human race. The smaller the number of parameters the easier the theory is to falsify. The following is a list of the phonological primes that Chomsky and Halle proposed for characterizing all the phonological systems of the world:

Major Class Features
 *sonorant
 *vocalic
 *consonantal
Cavity Features
 *coronal
 *anterior
 *round
 *distributed
 *covered
 glottal constriction
Secondary Apertures
 *nasal
 *lateral
Tongue Body Features
 *high
 *low
 *back
Source Features
 *voice
 *strident
 *heightened subglottal pressure

Manner Features
 *continuant
 *delayed release
 *primary
 *secondary
 supplementary
 suction
 velaric
 implosive
 *pressure
 velaric
 ejective
 *tense
Prosodic Features
 stress
 pitch
 *length

21

3.0.2 Chomsky and Halle based many of their features on phonetic phenomena with no regard for the semiotic value of these phenomena. They followed time-honored procedures for the most part, so, in order to implement a strong theory of markedness, it is necessary to question either the place in the system, the definition, or the validity of 23 of the 28 features proposed in SPE. I shall examine those features bearing asterisks; I have no comment concerning the rest. My aim is to reduce the number of primes and strengthen the hypothesis at the same time making the features phonetically and physiologically more accurate, thus increasing the observational, descriptive, and explanatory adequacy of the theory.

3.1.1.0 In this section I shall discuss the Major Class Features and their relationships to [continuant] and [nasal].

3.1.1.1 My first clue that something was wrong with the SPE D.F.'s came in work on Portuguese. Like other Romance languages, Portugue possesses an archetypical, balanced, apparently totally unremarkable segmental inventory. Such a system should be easily accounted for with a set of features that purports to be universal, yet neither those of SPE nor those suggested by Ladefoged (1971, hereafter PLP) can define a natural class for a morphophonemic rule of Portuguese nor can they define the consonantal syllable codas as a natural class. The canonical pattern of syllables in Portuguese is CV, with ony 4 consonants, /r, n, l, z/, and the glides, [y] and [w], capable of forming codas.[1] Mira Mateus (1975) specifies the consonants as:

	r	l	n	z	y	w
voice	+	+	+	+	+	+
ant	+	+	+	+	–	–
cor	+	+	+	+	–	–
cont	+	+	–	+	+	+
high	–	–	–	–	+	+

When I reviewed her work I felt that there were two errors in these specifications: 1. nasals specified as [–continuant], 2. the flap /r/, a sound incapable of prolongation, the most momentary sound of the language, specified as [+continuant]. Mira Mateus' specifications are inspired by Chomsky and Halle's description of [continuant] (317): "... sounds in which the primary constriction in the vowel tract is not narrowed to the point where the air flow past the constriction is blocked." As far as they were concerned, occlusion in the oral cavity made a segment [–continuant]. Their reasoning (318) on flaps as continuants is contorted and unconvincing.[2] The Portuguese segments in question are voiced, anterior, and coronal, yet these features do not define these segments as a class since they include /d/ [+voice, +coronal, +anterior, –continuent] which does not occur syllable finally in Portuguese. The feature [sonorant] (SPE: 302) excludes both /d/ and /z/ forcing syllable-final consonants to be described as:

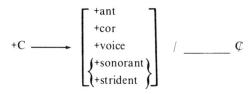

In order for this specification to work, it would have to be ordered before the rule of voiced consonant lenition whereby /b/, /d/, and /g/ become [ƀ], [đ] and [ǥ] since it suggests that [đ] may be syllable final, which is not the case. The disjunction in this rule suggests an underlying similarity that SPE D.F.'s are incapable of describing.

3.1.1.2.1 Do /r, l, n. z/ form a natural class? The SPE phonologist would have to say "no"; yet to the question "Is there an exclusive phonetic similarity in these segments?" a phonetician would answer "yes." The phonetic traits that unite all four consonants is their alveolar articulation and their continuous stream of egressive air. At no point in their articulation is the air stream completely occluded. The flap is a ballistic movement of the tongue against the alveolar ridge; this movement is not dependent on, nor does it occlude, the egressive air stream. We may describe these sounds as a natural class most easily and without disjunction if we discard the feature [continuant] for [occlusion], i.e. the *total* impedence of the air stream.

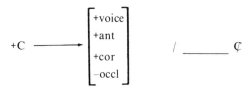

Now, syllable codas, the consonants /r, n, l, z/, and all the vowels can be described in a single statement.[3]

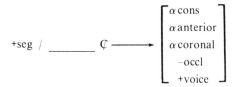

3.1.1.2.2 Wheeler, (1972: 92) remarks that "[continuant], though a manner of articulation feature, is required to define the basic category of stops." Indeed, linguists often find it necessary to refer to stops (the segments in which the egressive airstream is totally impeded) as a separate class, yet the only means they have for doing this using SPE D.F.'s is with negative specification of [continuant] and [sonorant]. Semiotically this is wrong since the stops in any language constitute a subset of the entire inventory. Indeed, SPE oriented phonologists often refer, informally, to the class of stops and fricatives using an ad-hoc feature [obstruent] because the phonetic primes they use do not provide a positive identity for these sounds. Stops impede the natural state of the vocal tract (breathing); and in a strong theory of marking, should be positively specified. Nasal consonants do not impede the air stream and should not be classified as stops.

3.1.1.2.3 Jakobson, Fant, and Halle (JFH) distinguish stops as (21) interrupted phones with "abrupt onsets" and "sharp wave front[s] preceded by periods of silence." Nasal consonants (considered [–continuant] in SPE) are characterized by JFH (39, 40, 52) as having vowel-like qualities, notwithstanding stop-like articulation in the oral cavity. JFH felt that redundant features could be eliminated from D.F. matrices and consequently never specified nasals as [∓interrupted] in their grids nor did they take any rigid stand on the character of these consonants (cf. Anderson, 1976: 328).

3.1.1.2.4.0 Apparent rationale for specifying nasal consonants as [–continuant] is found in Harms (1968: 33): "The nasal (stop) consonants are normally seen as phonetically non-continuant, thus allowing for nasalized (continuant) fricatives as well." The distinctive quality of nasal fricatives in any language is debatable; Chomsky and Halle (316) state that while:

> Ladefoged (1964, p. 24) reports that Twi has nasal affricates which contrast with both nasal and non-nasal plosives, we do not know of any certain examples of nasal continuants such as nasal [š] or [ž].[4]

3.1.1.2.4.1 The most elaborate defense of [continuant] (i.e. of nasal consonants as [–continuant]) appears in Anderson (1976) who acknowledges (328–329) that nasal consonants do not have the acoustic properties of stops. He maintains, however, that often stops and nasals may pattern similarly and may trigger similar operations and should be included in a natural class. He asserts (329):

> ... it is perfectly coherent ... to define non-continuant as ... articulated with a complete blockage in the oral cavity. This will delimit a class of

sounds including both the oral stops and the primary nasal consonants. It is then an empirical question whether this class is a useful, linguistically significant one, or whether we would rather prefer the class of sounds involving continuous airflow.

3.1.1.2.4.2 Anderson cites two examples in which nasals and stops (and in one case fricatives and sonorants) undergo similar modifications. He feels that a rule for this can only be written if nasals are specified as [–continuant].

A.1. The phoneme /k/ in Finnish supposedly spirantizes before oral stops and nasal consonants, i.e. before /t/ and /n/. He offers the following rule:

/k/ ——————→ /h/ / _____ [–cont]

Aside from the fact that this rule would spirantize /k/ before many more segments than /t/ and /n/, Anderson leads the reader astray with this datum and his rule. Except for the two verbs he cites, /näk–/ and /tek–/, /k/ only spirantizes before /t/. The spirantization of /k/ in these verbs (before /n/ and /k/) is considered an anomaly (cf. Campbell 1975, 15–16), yet Anderson uses them to defend his postulates (330):

> Just as this class [presumably /n, t/] is described by the feature [–continuant], defined as 'complete blockage of the oral cavity'. It would not, of course, be given by the specification 'blockage of airflow'. Thus we have a case in which the proposed definition of the feature [continuant] allows us to specify the environment of a phonological rule in a much more satisfactory way than would be possible under the alternative proposal.

A.2. Even the case of a /k/ that regularly spirantized before /t, n/ the feature [–continuant] is not necessary for generating this phenomenon. The rule:

$$k \rightarrow h \ / \ \underline{\hspace{2cm}} \begin{bmatrix} +\text{cons} \\ +\text{coronal} \\ \begin{Bmatrix} +\text{nasal} \\ -\text{voice} \end{Bmatrix} \\ -\text{strident} \end{bmatrix}$$

produces the desired effect using SPE Features and implies oral closure without commitment on the impedence of the egressive air stream. Of course the disjunction in this rule indicates that /t/ and /n/

are not members of a natural class. Nasal consonants are similar to stops only because egressive *oral* air is occluded, but nasals share the property of "continuous flow of air" with all other segments.

B. The other example he gives is the ". . . well known case of consonant lenition between sonorants in the Celtic language . . ." where (330):

    (a) Voiceless stops become voiced (/p t k/ →[b d g])
    (b) Original voiced stops become spirants (/b d g/ →[v ð g])
    (c) Voiceless continuants become voiced (/s ʀ ʎ/ →[z r l])
    (d) /m/ becomes a nasalized spirant [ṽ].

Anderson writes no rule in features to describe these changes; he even suggests that the voicing of /ʀ/ and /ʎ/ cannot be included if such a rule were written.

> It is clear that is /m/ is treated as a non-continuant, the weakening of consonants *other than dental sonorants* [my italics] can be described in a unitary fashion as follows: between sonorants, such consonants become voiced; if already voiced, they become continuant.

The formulation of such a rule would be something like:

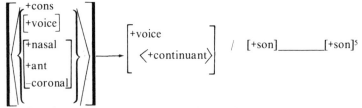

Anderson's exclusion of /ʀ/ and /ʎ/ is remarkable inasmuch as the following rule generates all the changes:

$$\left[\left(\begin{bmatrix}+\text{cons}\\[+\text{voice}]\\\left\{\begin{matrix}+\text{nasal}\\+\text{ant}\\-\text{coronal}\end{matrix}\right\}\end{bmatrix}\right)\right] \longrightarrow \begin{bmatrix}+\text{voice}\\\langle+\text{continuant}\rangle\end{bmatrix} \quad / \quad [+\text{son}]\underline{\qquad}[+\text{son}]^5$$

Friction is contingent on underlying voice and the only nasal to spirantize is /m/.

3.1.1.3 It is convenient, and often necessary, to refer to stops and nasal consonants as a natural class (segments with oral closure), but this should not be done at the expense of phonetic accuracy. All consonants are united by the feature "oral point of articulation" (cf. SPE, 302–303). In the event that nasal and occlusive consonants occasion similar phenomena in a particular language, the following specification will suffice to distinguish them from all other segments in the particular language:

$$
\begin{bmatrix}
+\text{consonant} \\
\left\{\begin{matrix} +\text{nasal} \\ +\text{occlusion} \end{matrix}\right\}
\end{bmatrix}
$$

Any closer association of nasal and stop consonants is misleading. In Jukun (Hill, unpublished), there is a three way contrast between occlusives, nasals and nasal occlusives:

/ba:/	'bag'	/ma:/	'salt'	/b̃à/	'give birth'
/da:/	'say'	/na:/	'cow'	/d̃à/	'be heavy'
/gà/	'think'	/ŋà/	'hate'	/g̃a:/	'try'

These segments can only be distinguished using the features [occlusion] and [nasal]. In addition, non-occlusive nasals nasalize a following vowel /ma:/→[mã:], /na:/——[nã:] and /ŋà/→[ŋã]. This can be regulated with the following rule:

$$
[-\text{consonant}] \longrightarrow [+\text{nasal}] \quad / \quad
\begin{bmatrix}
+\text{nasal} \\
-\text{occlusion}
\end{bmatrix}\underline{\hspace{2em}}
$$

The SPE specification of nasals as [–continuant] which unites them with stops, would force a linguist to consider the nasal stops of Jukun sequences rather than units.

3.1.1.4 By classifying all sounds with oral closure as [–continuant], linguists imply that the *only* difference between stops and nasals is the lowering of the velum and "sonorance". While these may be the only articulatory differences, the dynamic differences are so great as to indicate a serious shortcoming of a phonetic theory that claims similar air stream properties for stops and nasals. Notwithstanding their consonantal articulation, nasals may be prolonged and may constitute a syllable nucleus. Indeed all [–occlusion] segments share this property (even flaps may be lengthened into trills)[6]; [–occlusion] segments may be used to provide basic resonances on which tunes may be hummed or on which pitch variations may be superimposed. Occlusives, articulated by themselves using egressive pulmonic air, do not share these properties. Nasality may be superimposed on any oral vocoid, and nasal consonants are, like vowels, "naturally" voiced. The only affinities that "normal" nasal consonants have with stops is the major class feature [+consonantal] which implies a point of articulation in the oral cavity.

3.1.1.5 Do we loose anything by discarding [continuant] for [occlusion]? I have checked phonological systems of many different languages (see Appendix A) and no distinction has been lost. Nasal fricatives can be indicated as their oral counterparts plus nasality—ṽ or z̃ etc. Pre- or post-nasalized stops (see 3.4) would be specified as both occlusive and nasal with delayed transition of either the primary or secondary articulation if necessary. With [occlusion] as the distinctive feature of stops and affricates, the consonants divide as follows:

Stops and Affricates	~ everything else	+occlusion
Affricates	~ stops	+friction[7]
Fricatives	~ fricative	±slit[7]
Nasals	~ everything else	+nasality
Laterals	~ everything else	+lateral
/r/ (flap)	~ everything else	+consonantal
		–everything else

3.1.1.6 Seeing that nothing is lost by replacing [continuant] with [occlusion], what is gained? Specification of a natural class of syllable final segments in Portuguese is, perhaps, the least important desideratum of this change. The feature [+occlusion] provides: 1. a positive and unique specification for stops and affricates. 2. a greater level of observational adequacy, since this feature provides a means of recognizing that nasals have articulatory affinities with stops and air stream affinities with all other segments. 3. a strengthening of the D.F. hypothesis because by replacing [continuant] with [occlusion], the feature [sonorant] can be eliminated.

3.1.2 Chomsky and Halle define sonorants as (302) ". . . sounds . . . in which spontaneous voicing is possible . . . Sound[s] . . . with more radical constrictions than the glides, i.e. stops, fricatives, and affricates, are nonsonorant, whereas vowels, glides, nasal consonants, and liquids are sonorant." Chomsky and Halle contradict themselves because nasals and liquids have consonantal articulation; their oral articulation is more radical than that of glides. In the system advocated here, the class of vowels, glides, nasals, and liquids and approximants may be united as follows:

$$\begin{bmatrix} \text{-occlusion} \\ \text{-friction} \end{bmatrix}$$

The specification of a set of segments using independently motivated primes is more highly valued than the postulation of a prime to define a class of segments, especially in this case since [sonorant] includes more segments than it excludes, being a specification for both vowels and consonants. The elimination of [sonorant] from the D.F. inventory strengthens the hypothesis by a factor of 1 and it obviates the counter-intuitive specification of the glottal stop as a [sonorant] (SPE 303). The glottal stop can be specified as [-consonantal +occlusion].

3.1.3.0 Since nearly all phonological systems include the feature [nasal] and since nasals represent a synthesis of what has been traditionally referred to as "consonantal" and "vocalic" articulation, I consider them more basic to a D.F. hypothesis than the heading "secondary apertures" (see 1.1) suggests. Nasality is one of the major class features.

3.1.3.1 Grappling with consonants that can only be interpreted as units and which involve either prenasalization e.g.*mb*, post-nasalization *bm*, or mesonasalization *dnd*, Anderson[8] concludes (343):

> ... nasality occupies a peculiar status in the inventory of features. Though generally considered on a par with other features of manner of articulation, it is in some ways a suprasegmental, on a par with features of pitch. As a result the nasal consonants most generally found in the languages of the world are most naturally treated as oral stops on which a nasal pattern is realized: if the stop is nasal throughout, we get the common primary nasals, while 'contour' nasality patterns give rise to pre- and post-nasalized stops. The result is a theory of phonological and phonetic representation in which the segmental idealization is no longer quite so pervasive, since segments have internal structure which may be manipulated by rules.

The ability of the feature [nasal] to co-occur with (SPE) features such as [vocalic], [consonantal], etc. gives it a pervasiveness reminiscent of suprasegmentals, but some well-known suprasegmentals also involve laryngeal activity while nasality need not. Anderson recognizes (313) that the two types of nasal consonants (common primary nasals: *m, n, ñ*, etc. and pre- and post- as well as mesonasal stops) could be easily described using a feature such as [occlusion], but he argues in favor of [continuant].

3.1.3.2 A theory which includes [occlusion] can specify these unusual segments by combining the features: [occlusion, nasal, primary delayed transition, secondary delayed transition].

	mb	bm	bmb
occl.	+	+	+
nasal	+	+	+
D.T. 1°	–	–	+
D.T. 2 °	–	+	+

Nasality is considered to be the secondary articulation here since [+nasal] implies the presence of [–nasal] and not vice-versa. The *mb* order is the natural or unmarked combination of nasal and oral contoidal articulation, therefore neither D.T. 1° nor D.T. 2° is marked.

3.1.4.1.1 Chomsky and Halle's purportedly phonetic definitions of [vocalic] and [consonantal] do not help phonological theory. They define the class of [consonantal] segments as (302–303) ". . . sounds . . . produced with a radical obstruction in the midsagittal region of the vocal tract; . . . not every sound produced with a raised tongue is consonantal. The so-called retroflex vowels . . . are . . . non-consonantal." Rigorous work in phonetics has used the terms "consonant" and "vowel" to indicate patterning properties and the terms "contoid" and "vocoid" to indicate phonetic properties of segments. Pike (1947: 13–14) defines vocoids as ". . . any sound which has air escaping (1) from the mouth (2) over the center of the tongue (that is, not laterally) (3) without friction in the mouth (but friction elsewhere does not prevent the sound from being a vocoid)." He defines non-vocoids (i.e. contoids) as (24): ". . . any sound in which the air stream escapes from the nose but not the mouth; sounds in which air escapes from the mouth but over the side of the tongue [laterals]; sounds in which air escapes from the mouth but with friction in the mouth; and sounds during which the air stream has no escape." Abercrombie (1967: 170) states that "Their [contoid and vocoid's] rigorous definition is their great advantage; without it their usefulness is destroyed." Vocoid (the lack of oral) articulation corresponds to the "natural" state of the vocal tract in communication and is the backdrop for segmentation. Contoidal articulation involves impedence and should be considered the marked, positively specified, value. On a systematic level there is no need for both *contoid* and *vocoid* since *vocoid* is the negation of *contoid*. The distinctive feature hypothesis can be strengthened by the elimination of the SPE feature [vocalic] and hereinafter +C indicates [+contoid] (c.f. SPE: 302).

3.1.4.1.2 The class of sounds known as approximants (Catford: 119–127) is useful and, while not considered by Pike in his definitions of [vocoid] and [contoid], can be identified using the features advocated here. Approximants are ambivalent sounds; they may be vocoidal when voiced, but contoidal when voiceless because of the greater turbulence of air at the point of articulation caused by the increased velocity of the surd air stream (Catford: 120). Sounds such as [y], [w], [ɹ], [l], [i], and [u] are approximants. The common denominator of all of these sounds is the close approximation of the tongue to a point of articulation. The vocoids are [+high]. This close approximation creates redundant friction when the air is not subjected to laryngeal vibrations.

3.1.4.2.1 One of the uses of the feature [vocalic] has been the specification of semivowels *y* and *w* as [–cons] [–voc]. Chomsky and Halle suggest that the feature [syllabic] might. be an apt substitute for [vocalic]; it (354) "... would characterize all segments constituting a syllable peak ... vowels would normally be syllable peaks, liquids, glides, nasal consonants could become syllabic under specific circumstances." The latter set of segments constitutes the SPE class [sonorant] which has been eliminated from this inventory.

3.1.4.2.2 The syllable is a controversial linguistic unit. Chomsky and Halle's elevation of the concept to the level of a phonological prime has enabled linguists to attribute a distinctive function to syllable division. For example, a contrast such as Portugues *rio* [xí.u] 'river' vs. *riu* [xíw] 'he laughed' could be accounted for by considering the final segment of *riu* to be [–syllabic] whereas the final segment of *rio* could be characterized as [+syllabic]. Pulgram (1970: 65) does to believe the syllable to be a contrastive unit. He says: "The syllable is a unit ... whose phonological boundaries, ... are determined by a general set of phonological Rules [sic] ... of a given language." Being rule-produced it is non-distinctive. Catford (90) does not consider the contrastive power of the syllable, but defines it as "... a minimal 'chunk', or stretch of initiator activity, bordered by either minor, intra-foot, retardents, or by foot divisions themselves ..." Typical of initiator activity is a "power curve" which may be created by pulmonic, glottalic, and velaric air streams. Segments may be part of or may actually constitute a power curve.

3.1.4.2.3 The syllable is not really as difficult to define as Pulgram and his predecessors imagine, nor as primal as Chomsky and Halle seem to suggest. The traditional categories "consonant" and "vowel" have hindered rather than helped our understanding of the phenomenon known as syllabicity. Syllabicity is, essentially, the ability that a segment has to be articulated alone and be heard. Catford's definition suggests that movement of air initiated in the vocal tract is essential to syllabicity. Air stream initiation may be pulmonic, glottalic, or velaric. Using the pulmonic air stream, any non-occlusive segment can be articulated alone and be heard, thus any non-occlusive segment may be syllabic. Those segments we commonly call vowels are simply non-contoidal, non-occlusive, non-lateral, and non-fricative. Many languages allow syllabic [n̩], [r̩], [z̩], [š̩], [ž̩], etc. Beyond this, the glottalic and velaric air streams are supraglottal and require pressure, either positive or negative, to make ejectives, implosives, and clicks—all of which are audible when articulated in isolation. This pressure is achieved by contoidal articulation, thus the "vowel" or the vocoid is not an essential ingredient of the syllable nor is it a phonological prime. For languages which only use the pulmonic air stream the essence of the syllable is expressed in the following rule:

Potential Syllable Boundary Insertion-Pulmonic Air Stream

$$\emptyset \rightarrow \mathcal{C} \: / \: \text{_____} \qquad [-\text{occlusion}] \qquad \text{_____}$$

The universal essence of syllables is:

Universal Potential Syllable Boundary Insertion

$$\emptyset \rightarrow \mathcal{C} \: / \: \text{\_\_\_\_} \quad \left\{ \begin{bmatrix} [-\text{occlusion}] \\ \left\{ \begin{matrix} [\,+\text{glottalic}\,] \\ [\,+\text{velaric}\,] \\ \pm\text{suction} \end{matrix} \right\} \end{bmatrix} \right\} \quad \text{\_\_\_\_}$$

These rules state the minimal ingredients for syllables. Specific syllables in specific languages will have different and more complex configurations, but every syllable must have air stream movement, be it glottalic, velaric, or pulmonic.

3.1.4.2.4 I have claimed that all segments other than pulmonic occlusives can potentially constitute a syllable nucleus using the egressive air stream, that they may be articulated with no support and still be heard. Of course, the likelihood of their doing so in a particular language is inversely proportional to their degree of closure: *a* is the most likely candidate for a syllable nucleus, *i* less so, *l* less so, *s* idem, with virtually no likelihood that *t* or any other voiceless stop, which depend on support from a contiguous segment for their identity, can form a syllable peak. Certainly there are universal principles which determine the syllable shapes of strings of segments according to a sonority hierarchy which will be the converse of the strength hierarchy illustrated in Chapter VI of this work. In specific languages, rules may be written to account for the syllabation of strings of segments. Consider the following data.

Syllabation in Portuguese

Phonemic Sequence	Potential Syllables	Actual Syllables
anta	á.n.ta.	án.ta
farto	f.á.r.to.	fár.to
alto	á.l.to.	ál.to
palavra	pa.l.á.v.r.a.	pa.lá.vra
flor	f.l.ó.r.	flór
klauztro	kl.á.u.z.tr.o.	kláuz.tro
tranzasãũ	tr.a.n.z.a.s.ã́.ũ.	tran.za.sã́ũ
monztruozidade	m.o.n.z.tr.u.o.z.i.dá.di.	monz.tru.o.zi.dá.di
doido	dó.i.do.	dói.do
doído	do.í.do.	do.í.do
ruido	r.u.í.do.	ru.í.do
onra	ó.n.r.a.	ón.ra
ezlavo	e.z.l.á.v.o.	ez.lá.vo
pau	pá.u.	páu
perzpikaz	pe.r.z.pi.ká.z.	perz.pi.káz
sai	s.á.i.	sái
via	v.í.a.	ví.a
seio	s.é.i.o.	sé.io
saia	s.á.i.a.	sá.ia
saía	s.a.í.a.	sa.í.a
sei	s.é.i.	séi

The following rules account for the correct syllabation:

Rule 1.

$$\text{\cancel{C}} \rightarrow \emptyset \;/\; \begin{bmatrix} +\text{contoid} \\ \langle +\text{slit} \rangle \\ \alpha \begin{bmatrix} -\text{lateral} \\ -\text{fricative} \end{bmatrix} \end{bmatrix} \underline{\hspace{2cm}} \begin{bmatrix} -\text{contoid} \\ \left\langle \begin{matrix} +\text{contoid} \\ -\text{occl} \\ -\text{nasal} \end{matrix} \right\rangle \\ \alpha[+\text{friction}]\,[+\text{contoid}] \end{bmatrix}$$

This rule says A) no contoid shall have an independent air stream
initiation when followed by a non-contoid, $\text{\cancel{C}} \rightarrow \emptyset /$ [+contoid] _____
[–contoid]; B) when a fricative (only /z/ in Portuguese) is preceded by
/r/ or /n/ and followed by another contoid, there shall be no air
stream initiation solely with either segment:

$$\text{\cancel{C}} \rightarrow \emptyset \;/\; \begin{bmatrix} -\text{lateral} \\ -\text{fricative} \end{bmatrix} \underline{\hspace{2cm}} [+\text{friction}]\,[+\text{contoid}]$$

and C) when /f/ and /v/, the only slit fricatives in Portuguese, occur
before /r/ or /l/, a syllable boundary is deleted:

$$\mathcal{C} \rightarrow \emptyset \ / \qquad [\text{+slit}] \qquad \text{———} \qquad \begin{bmatrix} \text{+contoid} \\ \text{–occlusion} \\ \text{–nasal} \end{bmatrix}$$

Rule 1 eliminates the following potential boundaries:

		C A		B
á.n.ta.		f./l./ó.r.		pe.r./z.pi.ká.z.
A		A A		A
f./á.r.to.		kl./á.u.z.tr./o.		s./á.i.
		A A A		A
á.l.to.		tr./a.n.z./a.s./ã̃.ũ.		v./í.a.
A C A		A B A A		A
pa.l./á.v./r./a.		m./o.n./z.tr./u.o.z./i.dá.de.		s./é.i.o.
		A		A
do.í.do.		ó.n.r./a.		s./á.i.a.
		A A		A
dó.i.do.		e.z.l./á.v./o.		s./a.í.a.
A				A
r./u.í.do.		pá.u.		s./é.i.

Rule 2.

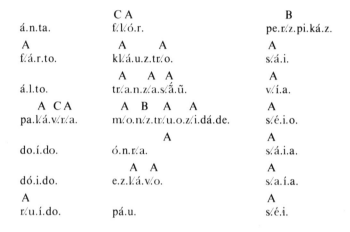

$$\mathcal{C} \rightarrow \emptyset \ / \qquad \left[\left\langle \substack{\text{+high} \\ \text{–stress}}_{*\mathcal{C}} \right\rangle \begin{smallmatrix} \text{–contoid} \end{smallmatrix} \right] \text{———} \left[\begin{smallmatrix} \text{+contoid} \end{smallmatrix} \left\langle \substack{\text{–contoid} \\ \text{–high}} \right\rangle \right] ([\text{+contoid}])\mathcal{C}$$

Rule 2 says A) delete a syllable boundary between a non-contoid
followed by one or two contoids after which there is a syllable
boundary; B)1) delete a syllable boundary either when a syllable initial
non-stressed high vowel is followed by a non-high vowel that is syllable
final or that precedes a syllable final contoid; or B)2) when a non-high
vowel is followed by a non-stressed high vowel that has a syllable
boundary or a contoid and a syllable boundary after it. Part B of Rule
2 is a mirror image rule that is right-to-left iterative. That is, it would
first scan a world like *saia* /sa.i.a./ and eliminate the second syllable
boundary /sa.ia/ which would make this word exempt from the mirror
image of the rule that eliminates syllable boundaries between a non-
stressed high vowel preceded by a non high vowel. The structural
description is not met.[9] Rule 2 finishes the syllabation of the Portuguese data:

2A	2A	2A 2A
á/.n.ta	fló/.r	pe/.rz.pi.ká/.z.
2A	**2B2 2A**	**2B2**
fá/.r.to	klá/.u/.z.tro.	sá/.i.
2A	**2A 2B2**	
á/.l.to.	tra/.n.za.sã́/.ũ.	ví.a.
	2A	**2B1**
pa.lá.vra.	mo/.nz.tru.o.zi.dá.de.	sé.i/.o
	2A	**2B1**
do.í.do.	ó/.n.ra	sa.i/.a.
2B2	**2A**	
dó/.i.do.	e/.z.lá.vo.	sa.í.a.
	2B2	**2B2**
ru.í.do.	pá/.u	sé/.i

These rules create syllables such as CV, CCV, XVCC and are probably fairly universal, since syllable structure in Portuguese is simple.

3.1.4.2.5 A problem may appear to exist concerning non-syllabic vocoids such as *y* or *w*, since the inventory of D.F.'s proposed here seems to have no way of distinguishing them from their syllabic counterparts, *i* or *u*. When their syllabic quality can be accounted for in a rule, as in the Portuguese data above, there is no problem: the sounds in question are distributional allophones of /i/ and /u/. On the other hand, a language may have a contrast between syllabic and non syllabic vocoids: [yá] ~ [i.á] ~ [ža] or [wé] ~ [u.é] ~ [g̵é]. I suggest that such contrasts, if they exist, may be accounted for with the following specifications:

	y	i	ž	w	u	g̵
contoid	–	–	+	–	–	+
widened glottis	+	–	–	+	–	–
high	+	+	+	+	+	+
palatal	+	+	+	–	–	–

The feature [widened glottis] corresponds to fortis articulation in contoids and lenis articulation in vocoids. (see 3.2.3., 1–4). The use of [+widened glottis] to distinguish [y] from [i] claims that glide articulation will be the same as that of lax vocoids. I am also claiming that *y* and *w*, when phonemic, are more highly marked than *i* and *u*, and that no language will contrast *yV* with *IV* or *wV* with *UV*. That is, no language will contrast a glide with a lax vowel followed or preceded by a non-lax vowel. This solution comes from Catford (165–6) who says: "... both the 'vowel' [i] and the 'semi-vowel' [j] involve an identical type of articulatory structure but ... [i] always has a noticeable duration whereas [j] is ... a rapid *glide* away from (or to) an approximant type structure."

3.2.0 In this section I examine SPE Manner Features.

3.2.1 The feature [continuant] has been replaced by [occlusion].

3.2.2.1 Chomsky and Halle associate the features [delayed release] 1° and 2° with the latter part of the articulation of a segment (318–319) yet nasals are initiated by a velic opening, itself a release, and are terminated by a velic closing. The term "delayed release" (primary and secondary) is misleading and inaccurate, since in the production of speech nothing is "released" in the stream of speech sounds which linguists analyse into segments. It is often objectively difficult to tell where each segment begins and ends; concatenations of articulatory gestures produce compromises in the vocal tract which cause contiguous sounds to round, to palatalize, velarize, etc. In addition, some sounds are so phonetically complex that the analyst must appeal to the dominant patterns in the language in order to decide whether they are units or sequences of units. Affricates, labialized, velarized, palatalized, rounded consonants, diphthongs, and nasal vowels often lend themselves to interpretation as sequences of segments rather than as units. When phonological analysis indicates that sounds such as these are units, a prime should indicate their unusual status through positive specification. The SPE features fail in this sector because, as Ladefoged points out (1971: 106): all continuants have a positive specification for [delayed release] in SPE.

3.2.2.2 Earlier (3.1.3.2 and 3.1.1.4) I suggested that the positive value which distinguishes complex units such as *č̆*, *j̈*, *kˣ*, *mb*, etc. from sequences is "transition" rather than release. This term will facilitate specification of units such as *mb*, *bm*, *bmb* as well as those which might be transcribed as *št* (cf. Catford, 1977: 212). The term "transition" identifies the subphonemic affrication which occurs in many languages when alveolar stops occur before high front vowels. These sounds do not make a clean break from occlusive to vocoidal articulation ([ti], [di]) when affricated ([tši], [dži]) rather there is an intermediate stage [+contoid], [+high], [+friction] which is halfway between vocoidal and occlusive articulation.

3.2.2.3 Another benefit of the feature [delayed transition] is the elimination of the feature [long]. Since we consider segments which could possibly be analysed as sequences of segments as possessing [delayed transition], long segments (often analysed as gemminates) will receive a positive specification for [delayed transition]. Both primary and secondary [delayed transition] will be necessary to distinguish between long and non-long affricates in languages such as Amharic. A complex contoid is considered to have a delayed release feature when both of its parts are contoidal: *bb̦, pp̦, ts, bm,* etc.. When contoids are labialized *k^w, t· ^w* etc., palatalized *p', t', k',* aspirated, or glottalized, *p̦,̦ ț,̦ c̦̦* they shall not be considered as having a positive specification for [delayed transition] since the added feature is non-contoidal. This solution allows segments which are, it is necessary to repeat, theoretical constructs rather than absolute articulatory reality, to remain completely unitary, contrary to the conclusions of Campbell (1974) and Anderson (1976).

3.2.3.1 Lass (1976, 39–50) argues that the qualities [tense] and [lax] have been defined impressionistically by theoreticians trying to maintain the three vowel height hypothesis. He asserts that the motor correlates for distinctions such as /i~I, e~ẹ, u~U, o~ọ/ in English are articulatory and can be described in terms of tongue position. Catford (1977: 199–208) has a similar opinion but suggests that there is (208) "... some justification for the retention of a parameter of tense/lax for the description of consonants. [but] For vowels such as parameter is dubious, ..." He indicates (203) that the only "tenseness characteristic" is a difference in intra-oral pressure which is achieved by glottal adjustment. In the production of contoids, the close approximation of articulator to the point of articulation, plus the greater volume of egressive pulmonic air thanks to a widened glottis which allows more air to escape produces what we call articulatory tension. Tension, then, is a feature concommitant with the feature [surd] (see 3.4.1 below) since the vocal bands are open. On the other hand, non-contoidal articulation is naturally voiced, that is, the vocal bands are close together. The "lax" vowels are articulated with a wider opening than their "non-lax" counterparts (cf. Catford, 1977: 204). This widening produces an inevitable lowering of intra-oral pressure. At the same time the glottis is widened, the subglottal pressure and the frequency of laryngeal vibrations is lowered.[10]

3.2.3.2 Glottal widening produces opposite and similar effects on contoids and non-contoids. Contoids with a widened glottal opening will have greater supraglottal pressure and will be "tense" whereas vocoids with a widened glottis will be "lax" owing to reduced laryngeal vibration caused by the greater opening. In both cases, a widened glottis contributes to a tendency that both types of segments share, the tendency towards voicelessness, e.g. the lenition of vocoids in languages such as Portuguese and English is a necessary precondition to their being devoiced.

3.2.3.3 The features [tense] and [lax] may be accounted for by the feature [(relatively) widened glottis] when such distinction as /i~I, e~ẹ, p~pʰ/ occur in languages. The feature replaces SPE [tense] and combines with the feature [glottal constriction] (SPE 315–316) which the authors use to account for the strong relatively unaspirated stops of Korean (Catford, 202) and for "creaky voice." See also Kim (1967, 1970).

3.2.3.4 It seems to be contradictory to consider a sound as having both a widened glottis and a constricted one. The glottis should be thought of according to its possible states. In the production of speech it is either involved in phonation or it is not. In the non-phonatatory state it is either closed or it is so open that no vibration occurs. In the phonatory state it may be widened slightly or the folds may be relaxed in such a way that it vibrates more slowly allowing more air to pass. A strongly aspirated segment such as a p^h has maximal glottal opening. A b has the glottis in a phonatory state. A strong but unaspirated stop such as *p has the vocal bands wider than for b but not so wide as for p^h. For a b^h their width and/or tension is between that of b and *p. Sounds articulated with laryngeal creak have the vocal bands in a quasi phonatory state. "Creak" is handled by the combination [+widened glottis], [+surd], [+glottal constriction]. The strong relatively unaspirated stops of Korean contrast with the aspirated and unaspirated voiceless stops as follows: (see also 3.4.3)

	*p	p^h	p
surd	+	+	+
widened glottis	+	+	−
glottal cons	+	−	−

3.2.4 The SPE feature [pressure] which the authors associate with velaric or glottalic air streams can be eliminated. Since we have assumed egressive air to be the unmarked state of the air stream, potential pressure is the natural state of phonetic production, since air is moved into the articulatory aparatus from an originator then moved outward, thus always creating potential pressure if the vocal tract is constricted. Pressure adds nothing to the distinctive capabilities of the inventory as we can see from the following specification:

	b	ɓ	p$^{?}$	kp	ṗ	ɓ$^{?}$
suction	−	+	−	−	+	+
glottalic	−	−	+	−	−	+
velaric	−	−	−	+	+	−

In other words, common stops, ingressives, glottalics, egressive velarics, clicks, and glottalized ingressives can be distinguished with no need for the feature [pressure], and thus the inventory is strengthened by the elimination of yet another feature.

3.3.0 In this section I shall deal with SPE features which the authors claim involve secondary apertures.

3.3.1 [Nasal] has been dealt with (3.1.1.3.2.2–3.3.2) and is located in the section Major Class Features.

3.3.2 The appropriate place for [lateral] ". . . sounds . . . produced by lowering the mid section of the tongue at both sides or at only one side. . ." (SPE: 317) (cf. 3.4.1) is with the Manner Features. The Secondary Aperture class may be eliminated.

3.4.0 In this section I shall deal with the source features, [voice] and [strident].

3.4.1 Laryngeal vibration [voice] is a parameter common to all phonological systems. It is the backdrop of communication, essential for the production of suprasegmentals. In most phonological systems voiced segments are more frequent than voiceless ones,[11] indeed some phonological systems, e.g. those of Dyirbal, Gadsup, or Nunggabuyu, have no voiceless sounds as systematic phonemes, all phonemes may be contrasted without invoking [voice]. (See Appendix A). I suggest that the marked value in any phonological system is voicelessness i.e. [surd] which shall be positively specified.[12]

3.4.2 Chomsky and Halle define stridents as having (329): '. . . greater noisiness than their nonstrident counterparts.' They claim that the sounds /ɸ/ and /f/; /β/ and /v/ in Ewe, as well as the sounds /θ/ and /s/ or /ð/ and /z/ of English are distinguished by stridency:

	ɸ	β	θ	ð	f	v	s	z
Continuant	+	+	+	+	+	+	+	+
Voice	−	+	−	+	−	+	−	+
Strident	−	−	−	−	+	+	+	+

Harris (1969a) questions the status of [strident] as a feature and hints that the phenomenon may be a redundant consequence of points and manners of articulation. The SPE features do not unite fricatives into a positively specified natural class. The feature [sonorant] is necessary to distinguish them from sounds such as *w, r, l*. Ladefoged (1971: 105–108) concludes that SPE D.F.'s do not handle fricatives adequately, having already stated (49) that ". . . the best solution is to distinguish between grooved and slit fricatives." Slit fricatives have (48) ". . . a wider articulatory channel and more doming (as opposed to hollowing) of the fore part of the tongue." The relative width of articulatory area accounts for relative presence of channel turbulence and high velocity of the air stream (cf. Catford, 1977: 24–46, 121–127, and 153–159). Fricatives may be distinguished from all other segments by the feature [friction] and among themselves, by the feature [slit], these two features replace SPE [strident], [distributed], ([continuant] having already been replaced by [occlusion]), and [sonorant] having been deleted. These features, [friction] and [slit], are manner features rather than source and cavity features.

3.4.3 The authors of SPE propose the feature [heightened subglottal pressure] (326) to specify the voiced aspirated stops of Hindi which are produced "without tenseness." They mention the possibility of setting up a "hyper feature" called "strength of articulation" alleging that ". . . certain facts such as the treatment of Spanish consonants in different contexts (see Harris, J., 1967) make this suggestion quite attractive." The feature [widened glottis] that I have proposed for replacement of tense-lax along with [surd] and [glottal constriction] account for the stops of Korean (see 3.2.3) as well as those of Hindi;

	*p	p^h	p	b	b^h	e	E	ẹ
surd	+	+	+	–	–	–	–	–
widened glot	+	+	–	–	+	–	+	+
glottal const	+	–	–	–	–	–	–	+

This obviates any need for a feature as unevinced (Lisker and Abrahamson 1971) as [h sg. pr.] which Chomsky and Halle use to specify these segments. The features [surd], [widened glottis], and [glottal constriction] suffice in describing the contrastive elements of the occlusive consonants of Spanish, English, Korean, and Hindi.

3.5.0 In this section I shall deal with the cavity features [coronal, anterior, round, covered] and the tongue body features collapsing them into a series called articulation features.

3.5.1 The SPE features mentioned above are used for specifying points of articulation:

	b	v	d	z	ẓ	ž	x̂	x	x̣	ħ	?
anterior	+	+	+	+	+	–	–	–	–	–	–
coronal	–	–	+	+	+	+	–	–	–	–	–
back	–	–	–	–	–	–	–	+	+	–	–
high	–	–	–	–	+	+	+	+	–	–	–
covered	–	–	–	–	–	–	–	–	–	+	–

The distinctions between labials, apico-alveolars, palatals, velars, retroflexes, and pharnygeals can be made without [coronal] and [anterior] by substituting [labial] for [coronal].

	b	v	d	z	ʐ	ž	x̂	x	x̣	ħ	?
labial	+	+	–	–	–	–	–	–	–	–	–
dorsal	–	–	–	–	–	–	+	+	+	–	–
palatal	–	–	–	–	–	+	+	–	–	–	–
high	–	–	–	–	+	+	+	+	–	–	–
slit	–	+	–	–	–	–	+	+	–	–	–
contoid	+	+	+	+	+	+	+	+	+	–	–
glottal const.	–	–	–	–	–	–	–	–	–	–	+

Studies of phonological systems and of phonological theory concur that apico-alveolar consonants are the most frequent; hence in the approach I advocate they should be the least marked. Consequently, they receive the fewest positive specifications which I accomplish by eschewing [coronal] for [labial]. The features [labial] and [dorsal] apply to both contoids and vocoids; the former indicates point of articulation for fricatives and stops without delayed transition, it may also indicate rounding of contoids as well as the rounding of vocoids.

3.5.2 The contrast between the vowels of *map* and *mop* [mäp], [map] in many dialects of American English suggests that a feature like [anterior] be maintained. I prefer to use [palatal], to specify both vocoids and contoids; indeed, I maintain that, whenever possible, distinctive features should specify both vocoids and contoids. (See Wang, 1968 and Naro, 1973, pp. 124–134.) Front vowels are [+palatal]. Palatal contoids ñ, š, ĺ, etc. are also [+palatal] and may be distinguished from retroflex contoids by this feature. The use of [palatal] and [dorsal] provides a negative specification for central vowels [–palatal, –dorsal].

3.5.3.1 The SPE tongue body feature [low] was used to distinguish vocoids ([±high], [±low]) in a three level system of vowel height. Since we regard the vowel *a* to be the segmental primitive, the unmarked value *par excellence*, and since this is traditionally regarded as a low vowel, we replace [low] with [raised] which indicates any movement of the tongue higher than the teeth.

3.5.3.2 The feature [raised] is useful in phonological descriptions. It is often necessary to distinguish alveolars and palatals from both velars and labials (see Pagliuca and Mowrey 1980). The specification [+raised, –dorsal] accomplishes this. In Baule, a language of the Ivory

Coast, the phoneme /w/ will front to [ẅ] after an alveolar contoid and a front vowel: /twi/ 'gun' [tẅi], /swi/ 'elephant' [sẅi], /lwi/ 'fat' [lẅi], /mucwe/ 'eight' [mucẅe] (Pagliuca and Mowry, 503). After labials and velars it does not change. Vago (1976) writes the following rule in SPE features to describe the process:

$$
\begin{bmatrix} -\text{cons} \\ -\text{syll} \\ +\text{round} \end{bmatrix} \longrightarrow [-\text{back}] \; / \; \left\{ \begin{bmatrix} -\text{syll} \\ \begin{bmatrix} +\text{coronal} \end{bmatrix} \\ \begin{bmatrix} -\text{back} \\ +\text{high} \end{bmatrix} \end{bmatrix} \right\} \underline{\hspace{1cm}} \begin{bmatrix} +\text{syll} \\ -\text{back} \end{bmatrix}
$$

Pagliuca and Mowrey illustrate Vago's rewriting of this rule using the JFH feature [grave], and then they use Wang's feature [labial], identifying the class of alveolars and palatals as [−labial, −back], which they are. Their rule is (504):

$$
\begin{bmatrix} -\text{cons} \\ -\text{syll} \\ +\text{round} \end{bmatrix} \longrightarrow [-\text{back}] \; / \; \begin{bmatrix} -\text{syll} \\ -\text{back} \\ -\text{labial} \end{bmatrix} \underline{\hspace{1cm}} \begin{bmatrix} +\text{syll} \\ -\text{back} \end{bmatrix}
$$

They object to this rule stating (504–505) that it "... obscures the true motivation of w-frōnting ... /w/ fronts to [ẅ] when surrounded by articulations which ... involve an active pulling forward of the tongue, which is the articulatory characteristic common to dental, alveolar, and palatal ... segments." Pagliuca and Mowrey do not recognize that a specification such as [−labial, −dorsal] identifies the common contoidal environment of the rule by negation of the other distinctive parameters in the Baule system. However, using the feature [raised] the fronting of /w/ after alveolars and palatals can also be regulated:

$$
\begin{bmatrix} -\text{contoid} \\ +\text{labial} \\ +\text{high} \end{bmatrix} \longrightarrow [+\text{palatal}] \; / \; \begin{bmatrix} -\text{back} \\ +\text{raised} \end{bmatrix} \underline{\hspace{1cm}} [+\text{palatal}]
$$

Also, in Baule /l/ is realized as [r] after alveolar and palatal contoids. While Pagliuca and Mowrey offer no rule in SPE features, an SPE rule would be:

$$[\text{+lateral}] \longrightarrow [\text{-lateral}] \quad / \quad \begin{bmatrix} \text{+consonant} \\ \left\{ \begin{array}{l} [\text{+coronal}] \\ \begin{bmatrix} \text{+high} \\ \text{-back} \end{bmatrix} \end{array} \right\} \end{bmatrix} \quad \underline{\hspace{3cm}}$$

Which can be written using the features advocated here as:

$$[\text{+lateral}] \longrightarrow [\text{-lateral}] \quad / \quad \begin{bmatrix} \text{+contoid} \\ \text{+raised} \\ \text{-dorsal} \end{bmatrix} \quad \underline{\hspace{3cm}}$$

The other data that Pagliuca and Mowrey illustrate comes from Fe?Fe? where reduplication of syllables creates a high vowel before any alveolar or palatal consonant followed by a front vowel or when any consonant is followed by a high front vowel. The rule they offer (508) for this is, in SPE features:

$$\begin{bmatrix} \text{+high} \\ \text{+back} \end{bmatrix} \longrightarrow [\text{-back}] \quad / \quad \underline{\hspace{1cm}} \left\{ \begin{array}{ll} (a) & C \quad \begin{bmatrix} V \\ \text{+high} \\ \text{-back} \end{bmatrix} \\ (b) & \left\{ \begin{array}{l} C \\ [\text{+cor}] \\ \begin{bmatrix} \text{-back} \\ \text{+high} \end{bmatrix} \end{array} \right\} \quad \begin{bmatrix} V \\ \text{-back} \end{bmatrix} \end{array} \right\}$$

Using the features advocated here, the same phenomenon can be described as follows:

$$\begin{bmatrix} \text{+high} \\ \text{+dorsal} \end{bmatrix} \longrightarrow [\text{+palatal}] \quad / \underline{\hspace{1cm}} \quad \begin{bmatrix} \text{+contoid} \\ \left\langle \begin{array}{l} \text{+labial} \\ \text{+dorsal} \end{array} \right\rangle \end{bmatrix} \quad \begin{bmatrix} \text{+palatal} \\ \langle \text{+high} \rangle \end{bmatrix}$$

This rule will front [ï] in the environment described for FE?Fe? If the class of segments that fronts vowels includes dentals (i.e. dentals, alveolars, palatals), the feature [raised] cannot be used. These articulations are identifed, and properly so, as [−labial, −dorsal, +contoid].

3.5.3.3 The feature [covered], (SPE 315) "... sounds produced with a pharynx in which the walls are narrowed and tensed and the larynx raised." has been used to indicate pharyngealized vocoids and contoids and to distinguish pharyngeal fricatives from other segments. Jakobson and Waugh (1979, hereafter J & W) have claimed (116, et passim) that no language distinguishes labialized from pharyngealized contoids or vocoids because both labial constriction or pharyngeal constriction create flat spectra and are indistinguishable. Iraqui Arabic does contrast /f/, /x/, /ħ/, and /h/ but these can be distinguished without a feature such as [covered]:

	f	x	ħ	h
fricative	+	+	+	+
contoid	+	+	−	−
glottalic constr.	−	−	−	+

This suggests that [covered] may be deleted from the D.F. inventory. Further evidence for the dispensibility of a special feature to indicate pharyngeal articulation comes from Egyptian Arabic which contrasts a set of plain alveolar stops and fricatives with pharyngealized ones /t, d, s, z/ ~ /t°, d°, s°, z°/ etc. The auditory impression that the pharyngealized segments give to learners unfamiliar with pharyngeal articulation is one of labiality (J&W, 116) and suggests that the alveolar contoids can be contrasted using this feature, [labial], and a rule of Egyptian Arabic will realize specifications such as [+occlusion, +raised, +labial] as pharyngeal in timbre rather than labial. The pharynx and the lips are opposite analogues of one another, just as the tongue tip and the uvula are. The latter make non-slit articulations for fricatives, flap articulations, and stops; the former may constrict the flow of air either as it enters or leaves the oral cavity. The pharynx is a set of internal, pre-oral lips. Using the features [contoid] and [labial] judiciously, contrasts can be made between labial, glottal, and pharyngeal fricatives, stops, and approximants, as well as between them and rounded and unrounded back and front vocoids:

	p	ꝑ	ƀ	px[13]	ħ	*[14]	u	ü	ï	i	h	?
contoid	+	+	+	−	−	−	−	−	−	−	−	−
friction	−	+	−	−	+	−	−	−	−	−	+	−
occlusion	+	−	−	+	−	−	−	−	−	−	−	+
labial	+	+	+	+	+	+	+	+	−	−	−	−
palatal	−	−	−	−	−	−	−	+	−	+	−	−
dorsal	−	−	−	−	−	−	+	−	+	−	−	−
glottal const.	−	−	−	−	−	−	−	−	−	−	+	+

Thus, [labial] indicates contraction of an extremity conduit, contoidal labiality indicates articulation at the lips, non-contoidal labiality may indicate rounding or pharyngealization of vocoids or contoids, depending on the language and the specific articulatory parameters.

3.6.1 I have finished my discussion of phonological primes without mentioning the segments referred to as 'r-sounds' (cf. Brakel, 1974). Because of the western European tradition of using the Roman Alphabet, we have come to associate a rather wide gamut of sounds with the grapheme 'r'. They range from the vocoids [ɹ] and [ə] to flap *r*, trills *r̃* and *R*, to *x*, *x̃*, *ɡ̆*, * g̃*, and *h*. The most unusual *r* is the Czech fricative trill /ꞔ/ about which Ladefoged (1971: 49) says: "What characterizes the Czech variant of the trill manner of articulation is that it is a laminal (and not an apical) trill, and the stricture is held for longer [sic] (but probably with a shorter onset and offglide)." In the system advocated here *r* sounds can be specified as follows:

	r	r̃	ꞔ	R	ɹ	ə	ɾ	ɽ
contoid	+	+	+	+	−	−	+	+
fric	−	−	+	−	−	−	−	−
slit	−	−	+	−	−	−	−	−
dorsal	−	−	−	+	−	−	−	−
widened glot.	−	−	−	−	−	−	−	−
high	−	−	−	−	+	−	−	+
raised	+	+	+	+	+	+	−	+
delayed trans.	−	+	+	+	−	−	−	−
palatal	−	−	−	−	−	−	−	−
Pos. Spec.	2	3	5	4	2	1	1	3

3.6.2 R-sounds represent a synthesis of contoid and non-contoid articulation. Retroflex *ɹ* is negatively specified for all parameters other than [raised] and [high], for the flap, *r*, [contoid] articulation is added; for the trill, delayed transition, for [ꞔ] [friction]; *R*, [dorsal]; ə is only [raised]. The similarity of *r, ɹ ,* and ə accounts for the allophonic variation that often occurs among these sounds within a single language. Since they are the ultimate synthesis of [contoid] and non-contoid, they are the last to appear, and, within the domain of [+contoid], the fact that *r* and *l* only differ by the feature [+lateral] helps explain why these sounds are in complementary distribution in many languages, and why they often develop into one another in many languages.

3.7 The D.F. inventory used in this approach, in order to facilitate the strong theory of marking is:

2 *Major Class Features:*	± contoid ± nasal
8 *Manner Features:*	± occlusion ± friction ± slit
	± lateral ± delay. trans. 1°
	± delay. trans. 2° ± widened glottis
	± glottal const.
5 *Articulation Features:*	± labial ± high ± raised
	± dorsal ± palatal
1 *Backdrop Feature:*	± surd
3 *Airstream Features:*	± velaric ± glottalic ± suction

——

19 primes

3.8 The strongest possible hypothesis about the sound systems of languages is that there is only one distinctive parameter. This hardly plausible hypothesis is easily reflected. The strength of a theory can be judged, however, as a function of this strongest hypothesis. The strength of a D.F. inventory as a linguistic hypothesis may be measured by the number of primes actually used divided into one. As the quotient increases, so does the strength of the hypothesis. The SPE inventory contained 25 features commensurate with those included here and, through the fraction $1/25$, those features give it a strength quotient of .04. The system I have indicated here has only 19 features giving it a strength quotient $1/19$ = .153. Dividing my quotient by the SPE quotient produces a quotient of .76, i.e., which means that my D.F. hypothesis is 24% stronger. In addition, I have made it more adequate as an instrument of observation and description and have brought it into line with a strong theory of marking. The comparison that I have just made between two hypothetical inventories suggests, as well, as means of comparing the complexity of phonological systems: one simply compares the number of features necessary to specify the systematic phonemes of both systems. Phonological complexity, or the markedness of a particular system can be measured by the quotient of the smallest number of D.F.'s needed to specify a phonological system, divided into the number needed for the system in question. Beyond this, the generative power of this theory, the inventory proposed here, 2^{19} or 524,288 separate distinctive segments, is considerably less, 1.6% of that of the SPE D.F.'s: 2^{25} or 33,554,432 potentially distinctive segments. While the reduction of the number of phonological primes in the revised inventory makes it a stronger hypothesis and explanatorily more adequate, the descriptive and observational adequacy of these primes must be examined. To some extent this has been done in this chapter. Chapter V and Appendix A contain further examination of the descriptive and observational adequacy of the revised phonological primes.

Footnotes

[1]One could unite these with a language-specific feature as Lass does for English (168–212), but a proliferation of ingredients weakens the hypothesis contained in a distinctive feature inventory.

[2]Harris (1969: 46) is very reluctant to accept this specification for the flap /r/ of Spanish.

[3]Syllable division in Portuguese is accomplished by a rule and [y] and [w] need not enter the segmental phonemic inventory.

[4]Ladefoged's examples are of *prenasalized* affricates. Catford (1977: 147) identifies an "endolabiodental nasalized fricative [ṽ]" for English in words like *triumph* and *triumvirate*.

[5]In these rules I use SPE features to show that they can be written in the framework Anderson used. Using the features advanced in this section, these phenomena may be expressed in the following rule:

$$
\begin{bmatrix} \left\langle \begin{matrix} [+contoid] \\ [-surd] \\ \left\langle \begin{bmatrix} +nasal \\ +labial \end{bmatrix} \right\rangle \end{matrix} \right\rangle \end{bmatrix} \rightarrow \begin{bmatrix} [-surd] \\ \left\langle \begin{matrix} -occlusion \\ +friction \end{matrix} \right\rangle \end{bmatrix} \bigg/ \begin{bmatrix} -occl \\ -fric \\ -surd \end{bmatrix} \underline{\hspace{2cm}} \begin{bmatrix} -occl \\ -fric \\ -surd \end{bmatrix}
$$

[6]Catford (1977: 130) maintains that trills are not prolonged flaps, although later (196) he admits [length] as a phonological distinguishing factor between sounds such as Portuguese /r/ and /r̄/.

[7]See section 3.4.2.

[8]Anderson could have done his readers a great service by identifying languages in which mesonasalization occurs. In the 700 phonological systems described by Ruhlen, not a single case of mesonasalization appears.

[9]I owe this formulation to Ken Hill of the Linguistics Department at the University of Michigan.

[10]Catford (205) criticizes the assertion that "lax" vowels with a more open glottis have a lower subglottal pressure as an account for their shorter duration than that of "tense" vowels. He says: "The English lax vowel /I/, for instance, under certain conditions of intonation can be extremely long: for example "he did"? [hi   dI: : :d], with a rising-falling—tone on 'did', expressing astonished inquiry." In my speech, this rising-falling-rising tone occurs with a laryngeal creak produced by a widened glottis. The prolongation of a "lax" vowel is appropriate for an utterance which expresses "astonished

inquiry." It is a phonatory-gesticulatory analog of an unexpected event. Catford's point is, simply, that "lax" vowels can be lengthened.

[11]Catford (1977: 107) supports this assertion although he indicates that voiceless segments outnumbered voiced in a phoneme count of Cantonese. He neglected to mention whether tonemes were included; certainly voiced segments and tonemes which entail laryngeal resonance would have outnumbered voiceless segments.

[12]English speakers may be reluctant to accept voicelessness as the designator of a marked feature because of the cumbrous nature of the word. They should note, however, that voicelessness is the marked form, it implies voice in other segments. I have adopted [surd] here because of its simplicity and convenience.

[13]This sound is a pharyngeal stop.

[14]This sound is a pharyngeal approximant.

Chapter IV
Acoustic D.F.'s and the
New Postulates

4.1 Chomsky and Halle's inventory of D.F.'s grew out of an earlier hypothesis which was first illustrated in Jakobson, Fant, and Halle's *Preliminaries to Speech Analysis* (hereafter PSA). Generativists discarded these primes, which are based on acoustic data, as the emphasis of linguistic study shifted from perception of language to its production and, in this case, the production of sound in language. J&W recently (1979) defended the acoustic postulates and steadfastly insisted that communication is achieved by sound and not by its production, the study of which they regard as (83) "... a crude metrical attitude [opposed to their] ... sane, relational, topological treatment." They maintain that sufficiently distinctive spectral configurations of the sounds of a language can be produced using articulatory gestures that are quite different from the ones linguists have considered to be standard for a particular language. They go so far as to assert (96–7) that a tongue is not even necessary to produce intelligible speech. Certainly J&W cannot be claiming that tongueless speech, regardless of its intelligibility, which certainly must depend on both the good will and close attention that listeners would have when trying to understand the speech of a tongueless person, sounds anything like normal speech. Regardless of the preferability of acoustic primes over articulatory ones, both the JFH inventory and the one I have proposed are theories of the speech sounds of language; both have a distinct generative capacity and can be compared vis à vis their power as a generative mechanism, their adequacy as descriptive tools, and their simplicity as a theory of human speech—which is the object of this chapter.

   4.2.0 The features JFH proposed in PSA are [1 vocalic, 2 consonantal, 3 interrupted, 4 checked, 5 strident, 6 voiced, 7 compact, 8

49

grave, 9 flat, 10 sharp, 11 tense, 12 nasal]. They contrast with their negations i.e. [1 –vocalic, 2 –consonantal, 4 –checked, 6 –voiced] or with other features: [3 interrupted-continuant, 7 compact-diffuse, 9 flat-plain, 10 sharp-plain, 11 tense-lax, 12 nasal-oral]. For the purposes of this paper, I shall consider the original 12 to contrast with their negations. In the following paragraphs I present the definitions of the acoustic primes.

4.2.1 [vocalic] "Vowels have no obstructive barrier along the median line of the mouth cavity ... (PSA, 19) Phonemes possessing the vocalic feature have a single periodic ('voice') source whose onset is not abrupt ... the vocalic formants have small dampening ... [expressed] in the narrow bandwidth of the formants ... the lower formants have greater intensity." (PSA, 18–19). In PSA, the authors did not consider the possibility of the phonemic status of surd vowels which contrast with voiced vowels in languages such as Comanche, Ute, Mayan Chontal, Gulla, Teso, and Bagirmi (J&W, 135). This admission obliges J&W to resort to the syntagmatic definition of vowels as (85) "... the most usual carriers of syllable nuclei ..."

4.2.2 [consonantal] "... consonants have a barrier sufficient to produce either complete occlusion or a turbulent noise sound. (PSA, 19–20) Phonemes possessing the consonantal feature are acoustically characterized by the presence of zeros that affect the entire spectrum." (19) This appears to mean that the sound spectra of consonants are less evenly textured than those of vowels. The authors, (JFH, 19) and (J&W passim) claim that the class of sounds known as liquids, *r*'s and laterals, are both vocalic and consonantal although their intensity is lower than that of the vowels. Glides (*h* and *?*), they claim, are neither vocalic nor consonantal. They lack the harmonic source of vowels and zeros in the spectra. Sounds commonly represented as *y* and *w* are not considered glides, but non-syllabic vowels, (PSA, 20).

4.2.3 [Interrupted] "The abrupt onset distinguishes the interrupted consonants (stops) from the continuant consonants (constrictives) ... Stops ... [have] a sharp wave front preceded by a period of complete silence, ..." (21). JFH consider liquids to be of 2 sorts: [continuant] such as *l*, *ł*, etc. or [interrupted] such as the flap. They consider the English /r/ to be a type of schwa (22).

4.2.4 [Checked] "In spectrograms ... checked phonemes are marked by a sharper termination ... The air stream is checked by the compression or closure of the glottis."

4.2.4 [Strident] "Sounds that have irregular waveforms are called *strident* ... oscillograms show a distinctly higher periodicity and uniformity in mellow constrictives [i.e., –interrupted] such as /θ/ in comparison with /s/ and other strident constrictives. Strident phonemes are primarily characterized by a noise which is due to turbulence at the point of articulation ... a supplementary barrier that offers greater resistence to the air stream is necessary ... [for the production of] stridents." (23–4)

4.2.5 [Voiced] "The most striking manifestation of 'voicing' is the appearance of a strong low component which is represented by the voice bar along the base of the spectrogram ... Voiced phonemes are emitted with constant periodic vibrations of the vocal bands ..." (26)

4.2.6 [Compact] "Compact phonemes are characterized by the relative predominance of one centrally located formant region (or formant). They are opposed to diffuse phonemes in which one or more non-central formants or formant regions predominate ... consonants articulated against the hard or soft palate (velars and palatals) are more compact than the consonants articulated in the front part of the mouth ... open vowels are the most compact, while close vowels are the most diffuse." (27)

4.2.7 [Grave] "... this feature means the predominance of one side of the significant part of the spectrum over the other. When the lower side of the spectrum predominates, the phoneme is labeled grave; when the upper side predominates, we term the phoneme acute ... gravity characterizes labial consonants as against dentals, as well as velars vs. palatals and, similarly, back vowels articulated with a retraction of the tongue vs. front vowels with advanced tongue." (30).

4.2.8 [Flat] "Flattening manifests itself by a downward shift of a set of formants or even of all the formants in the spectrum ... Flattening is chiefly generated by a reduction of the lip orifice (rounding) ... Instead of the front orifice of the mouth cavity, the pharyngeal tract, in its turn, may be contracted with a similar effect of flattening." (31)

4.2.9 [Sharp] "This feature manifests itself in a slight rise of the second formant and, to some degree, also of the higher formants ... the oral cavity is reduced by raising a part of the tongue against the palate." (31)

4.2.10 [Tense] "... tense phonemes display a longer sound interval and a larger energy ... tense phonemes are articulated with greater distinctness and pressure than the corresponding lax phonemes." (37–8)

4.2.11 [Nasal] "The spectrogram of nasal phonemes shows a higher density than that of the corresponding oral phonemes ... between the first and second vowel formants there appears in the nasal vowels an additional formant with concommitant weakening in the intensity of the former two ... the nasal consonants add a ... murmur ... [which] possesses two constant and clear formants, one at about 300 cps. and the other at about 2500 cps." (39–40)

4.3.1 Contrasting the JFH features with the ones advocated here (see Appendix C) establishes the following as equivalents:

JFH	Brakel
sharp	palatal
consonant	contoid
interrupted	occlusive
nasal	nasal
checked	glottal constriction
voiced	surd
tense	widened glottis

The features [DT 1°, DT 2°, suction, glottalic, velaric] are not commensurate with anything proposed by JFH. DT 1° and 2° are prosodic features, features that are superimposed on the properties of a sound, either from an articulatory or acoustic point of view, when the sound is analyzed as being a long or complex segment instead of a sequence of segments. *Suction, glottalic,* and *velaric* are air stream features not taken into consideration by JFH, but certainly important in the characterization of distinctive sound used in the languages of the world. The remaining features to be contrasted are:

JFH	Brakel
vocalic	lateral
strident	fricative
compact	slit
grave	labial
flat	raised
	high
	dorsal

That is, where commensurate, my system has two more features than the acoustic set, and either my system can be trimmed by two, or the JFH system is lacking in two.

4.3.2 JFH proposed to distinguish laterals and *r* sounds (liquids) in the following manner:

	l	ȴ	ɨ	ɬ	tl	r	ɹ	r̃	R	ř
consontal	+	+	+	+	+	+	−	+	+	+
vocalic	+	+	+	+	+	−	+	−	−	−
grave	−	−	+	−	−	−	−	−	+	−
sharp	−	+	−	−	−	−	−	−	−	−
strident	−	−	−	+	−	−	−	−	−	+
interrupted	−	−	−	−	+	+	−	−	−	−

There are several contradictions in these specifications. 1) Notwith-standing the claim of (PSA, 19) that laterals and *r* sounds have both the consonantal and vocalic features, the major means of distinguish-ing between them is to use the feature [vocalic] to identify laterals as opposed to *r* sounds and the other consonants which are [–vocalic]. JFH also assert (26) that despite the high dampening of the formants of fricative laterals and *r*'s, both retain acoustic traits of liquids, they are liquids with superimposed stridency. Their specification is incon-sistent with this statement. 2) JFH proposed to distinguish /r/ and /l/ (the flap and the alveolar lateral) by the feature [interrupted]. In a language such as Portuguese /r/ and /l/ contrast with /d/ inter-vocalically: *mora* 'he dwells', *mola* 'spring', *moda* 'style' and with /i/ and /u/ post-consonantally, *prazer* 'pleasure', *placa* 'license plate', *piano* 'piano', *pueril* 'puerile'. The contrast of these segments can only be maintained by the following specifications in JFH D.F.'s.

	l	r	d	i	u
interrupted	–	+	+	–	–
consonantal	+	+	+	–	–
vocalic	+	⊕	–	+	+

I have placed a circle around the + for [vocalic] as a specification for /r/. In order to contrast /r/ with /d/, /r/ must be specified as such, but such a specification [+interrupted, +vocalic] makes it a peculiar sound indeed, given that Jakobson considers vocalic sounds to be syllable nuclei. If one were to specify /r/ as [–interrupted], on the other hand, it would no longer contrast with /l/. The flap /r/ should be classified as I have recommended, as a contoid which is negatively specified for every distinctive parameter other than [raised], making it the least marked of contoids. This leaves [vocalic] as the sole distinc-tive feature of laterals according to the JFH approach, since they are both consonantal and vocalic. I suggest, then, that [lateral] be accepted as an apt substitute for [vocalic]. All non-contoids will be [–lateral] whereas a subset of the contoids, the laterals, will receieve a positive mark for laterality, their unique trait. This has not reduced the number of different features, it has just replaced one for another.

4.3.3 The PSA features [grave], [flat], and [compact] (along with [sharp] which corresponds to my [palatal]) reflect different points of articulation as well as different configurations of sound spectra. They correspond to my features [labial], [dorsal], [high], and [raised] and distinguish a total of 16 apertures and points of articulation as opposed to the 29 distinguished by my system.[1] A comparison of how the two systems characterize vocoids will be revealing.

Brakel System—Vocoid Distinction

	Front								Central				Back							
	i	ü	I	e	ö	ę	ǫ̈	ä	ɨ	ɘ	â	a	u	ī	U	o	ë	ǫ	ę̈	A
labial	-	+	-	-	+	-	+	-	-	-	-	-	+	-	+	+	-	+	-	-
palatal	+	+	+	+	+	+	+	+	-	-	-	-	-	-	-	-	-	-	-	-
high	+	+	+	-	-	-	-	-	+	-	-	-	+	+	+	-	-	-	-	-
raised	+	+	+	+	+	+	+	-	+	+	+	-	+	+	+	+	+	+	+	-
wide glot.	-	-	+	-	-	+	+	-	-	-	+	-	-	-	+	-	-	+	+	-
dorsal	-	-	-	-	-	-	-	-	-	-	-	-	+	+	+	+	+	+	+	+

PSA System—Vocoid distinction

	i	ü	I	e	ö	ę	ǫ̈	ä	ɨ	ɘ	â	a	u	ī	U	o	ë	ǫ	ę̈	A
compact	-	-	-	-	-	-	-	+	-	-	-	+	-	-	-	-	-	-	-	+
grave	-	+	-	-	+	-	+	-	-	-	-	-	+	+	+	+	+	+	+	+
flat	-	+	-	-	+	-	+	-	-	-	-	-	+	-	+	+	-	+	-	-
sharp	+	+	+	+	+	+	+	+	-	-	-	-	-	-	-	-	-	-	-	-
tense	+	+	-	+	+	-	-	+	+	+	-	+	+	+	-	+	+	-	-	+

The problem with the PSA specifications is that they do not contrast the high vowels *i, u* with *e, o* nor the high lax vocoids, *I, U* with *E, O*—unless one considers the latter to be [+compact], i.e. low. In addition, they do not contrast the central vocoids, *ɨ, ɘ* , and *â* from one another in any convincing manner. About the lack of a mark to distinguish *e* from *i*, etc., J&W say the following (131): "It must be remembered . . . that . . . the geometric mean /e/ . . . is noncompact in relation to the compact /ä/ and nondiffuse in relation to the diffuse /i/ . . ." Earlier, they have claimed ". . . we are, actually, clearly faced in these cases with the bifurcation of the binary opposition diffuse ~ compact and nondiffuse ~ diffuse." They have, in other words, either raised *diffuse* to the level of distinctive feature or they have abrogated the strictly binary nature of their feature system. In order to maintain strict binarity, it is necessary to add another prime to their inventory in order to distinguish high and mid vowels. Their alternative is to abrogate the principle of binarity which they adamantly insist upon as correct and the only way to describe communication (cf. J&W 23–4, 81–2, 146, 173–4). This makes the two systems the equivalent of one as far as their generative capacity of point of articulation and degree of aperture is concerned.

4.3.4 The PSA features contain the feature [strident] which is used to contrast sounds such as *Ө* from *s*, *x* from *X*, the former being [–strident] (mellow) and the later [+strident]. Unfortunately, PSA has no means of distinguishing contrasts between *p* and *f* or *b* and *v* the latter of which occurs in Continental Portuguese: *Cabo* [kábu] 'handle' *cavo* [kávu] 'I dig';[2] since both *b* and *v* are non-strident. Other languages that maintain contrasts between *b* and *v* are Béni (Wescott, 1965), Mbembe (Barnwell, 1969), Etskato (Laver, 1969) and Ewe (Berry, 1951). I have distinguished these phonemes by considering *f, v, Ө, d, š* and *x* to be slit fricatives and *b, s, ṣ,* and *X* to be non-slit. That is, the fissure at the point of articulation is not preponderantly horizontal. The /*b*/ of some languages may be an approximant, i.e. a labial contoid which may have audible local friction only when there is no laryngeal impedence. In this case it would be specified as [+contoid, +labial, –friction], in the case that there was audible friction when voiced, it would be positively specified for [fricative] but not for [slit]. It may be concluded that there is a need to distinguish, within the contoids known as fricatives, two subsets, one characterized by slit articulation, the other not. Non-slit fricative articulation *within the oral cavity* produces the stridency noted by JFH etc., whereas labial fricative articulation produces a mellow fricative, regardless of whether the articulation is labio-dental [slit] or bilabial [–slit].

4.4 It has been shown that in order for the PSA features to distinguish contrasts linguists know exist it is necessary to add two features, [raised] and [slit], to the inventory. This makes the system JFH propose the equivalent of the one proposed here. Fudge (1967, 4) has said "It is thus dangerous and misleading to say that either articulatory or auditory feature ARE the phonological elements, unless they correlate so closely that no facts of language are obscured by treating them as if they were the same: . . ." Concerning the powers of specification of the revised acoustic primes and those I suggest, they appear to be near equals. A further test of their equivalence will come in the following chapter, where strength hierarchies of segmental types will be contrasted.

Footnotes

[1]The articulatory primes that I have proposed, [palatal, labial, dorsal, raised, high] do not have a generative power of 2^5 or 32 points of articulation because no segment can be [+high, –raised], so three units must be subtracted giving it a generative power of 29 points of articulation.

[2]A phonological analysis of some dialects of Portuguese would identify [ƀ] as an allophone of /b/. In some dialects, however, the non-occlusives [ƀ, đ, ǥ] are preponderant—they only occur as occlusives after a homorganic nasal. In other words, these phonemes may be identified as fricatives rather than occlusives since their occlusive realization is definitely a minority.

Chapter V
Segmental Strength, Hierarchies, and Phonological Primes[1]

5.1.0 Linguists have felt that the segments that occur in languages have a relationship of relative strength. Hooper (1975) offers a strength hierarchy similar to the following one as a strategem for explaining the tautosyllabic distribution of segments (cf. 206):

Segment Type	Relative Strength	Value
Voiceless Occlusives	High	6
{Voiceless Non-Occl. / Voiced Occlusive}	Less High	5
Voiced Non-Occlusive	Less High	4
Nasals	Weak	3
Liquids	Weaker	2
Glides	Weakest	1

She considers the optimal distribution of segments in the syllable to be:

Margin	Nucleus	Margin
Obstr.-Nasal-Liquid-	Glide-Vowel-Glide -	Liquid-Nasal-Obst.
Least Vowel-Like	Most Vowel-Like	Less Vowel-Like
Strong	Weak	Weak

Suggestions such as this abound in the literature in which linguists have attempted to define the syllable on phonetic grounds. This pattern and the hierarchy she proposes as well as their congeners seem correct from a phonetic point of view, yet Hooper takes no position concerning physical correlates to the hierarchy. She views strength as

57

(198) a "... cover feature ... [a] theoretical construct, not entirely divorced from physical reality, ... but ... [whose] importance is seen only in ... [its] function in a linguistic system." For this reason she determines her hierarchy on "phonological" grounds which are functional and dynamic.

5.1.1 *Strong position.* The number of contrasts in a particular position determines the relative strength of such a position. Hooper uses the Spanish syllable as an example showing that all phonemes in that language contrast syllable initially which suggests to her that syllable onsets are the strongest position from which it follows that initial position is the natural position for strong consonants.

5.1.2 *Weak position.* Positions within the syllable in which relatively few phonemes contrast are weak. In most languages fewer consonants contrast in syllable final position, so, she reasons, syllable final position, a weak position, is the ideal place for weak consonants.

5.1.3 *Reduction of contrasts.* Hooper uses the Spanish syllable as an example of this phenomenon. Different registers of that language allow a greater or smaller number of consonants to contrast syllable finally. Most "formal" or "academic" varieties permit up to 15 consonants syllable finally: / p t k, b d g, f, Θ, s, x, r, l, n/ as well as the clusters / ns, rs, ks/. Some "folk" varieties only permit 6: /(Θ), (d), r, l, s, n/ while others delete all syllable final contoids. While Hooper fails to mention it, the stronger segments are most readily deleted in this position.

5.1.4 *Neutralization of contrasts.* Positions in which contrasts are neutralized are weak positions. Contrasts such as [±surd], [±high], [±occlusion], and [±delayed transition] are often neutralized syllable finally.

5.1.5 *Susceptability to deletion.* The greater likelihood that a segment may be deleted is an indication of its relative strength. Hooper claims that historical evolution of the type verified in Iberian Romance: *tt>t; t>d; d>đ; đ>∅*; suggests that voiceless stops are stronger than voiced and so on.

5.2.0 Foley (1977) postulates a set of primes of phonological strength which he derives from (25) "... thoughtful considerations of natural language." and from the examination of phonological processes. These primes are:

5.2.1 *Propensity towards spirantization.* The weaker segments have a greater tendency to spirantize. He assigns number values to the segments as follows: strong (labials) – 3; medium (dentals) – 2; weak (velars[2]) – 1.

5.2.2 *Segmental strength.* Geminate voiceless stops are the strongest, then voiced stops, then voiced fricatives:[3] *kk – 4, k – 3, g – 2, g – 1.*

5.2.3 *Degree of resonance.* This is the propensity that a segment has for vocalization: stops are least likely, non-occlusive, non-fricative segments are most likely: r – 5, 1 – 4, n – 3, s – 2, t – 1.[4]

5.2.4 *Binding strength.* Sequences of segments, e.g. *kw*, are weakest, doubly articulated segments are stronger, e.g. *k^w*, and units, e.g. *p*, are strongest:[5] sequence – 1, complex unit – 2, unit – 3.

5.2.5 *Vowel strength.* 1. High vowels are weakest and low are strongest: high – 1, mid – 2, low – 3.

5.2.6 *Vowel strength* 2. Front vowels are weak and back are strong: front – 1, back – 2.

5.2.7 Foley seems to regard the total strength of segments to be the sum of the number values of his theoretical primes (cf. 45, 90), yet his primes do not combine into a coherent system which establishes strength relationships among classes of segments.

5.3 There are many shortcomings to both approaches to segmental strength. Despite his admonitions against "phonetic reductionism" (25) Foley's parameters may be directly correlated with articulatory gestures. Even though Hooper's attempt seems to be the better of the two and her hierarchy of segmental strength seems intuitively correct, it is disturbing that diachronic evidence from only 4 languages (Spanish, Icelandic, Pali-Sanskrit, and Ijo) suffices for her to claim that her hierarchy is universal. It is even more disturbing that she suggests no articulatory correlates for a hierarchy whose members (including the glides) are articulatorily defined. Both researchers' avoidance of articulatory considerations stems from the parameters with which they view phonology. This avoidance is inappropriate because all phonological systems have an articulatory origin, they are products of the (universal) human vocal tract which is regulated by the brain. Neither approach defines segmental strength; each only amasses sets of disparate behavioral characteristics which the authors take to reflect the strength of segments.

5.4.1 Segments themselves are only constructs or artifacts that linguists use to transcribe speech. They are signs which denote complex articulatory gestures imperfectly, but, in phonemic transcription, in a manner sufficient to represent distinctive phonic elements used in transmitting messages. Indeed, segments are as theoretical as Hooper and Foley feel that strength is, but strength is not difficult to define. It is a combination of the amount of impedence applied to the supraglottal egressive air stream, the number of facultative resonance chambers used, and deviation from the voiced state of the glottis.

5.4.2 I assume egressive air and laryngeal resonance to be basic to the act of speaking. All languages employ egressive pulmonic air; all languages have voiced segments; all have suprasegmentals requiring laryngeal resonance; and primative communication, crying, involves laryngeal resonance. The ubiquity of voice in human communication suggests that voicelessness is the marked state. The ubiquity of egressive pulmonic air flow in human communication suggests that impediments or deviations from this state represent markedness—the greater the deviation and the greater the impediment(s), the greater the strength or the markedness of the segments involved. By way of illustration, compare the amount of force involved in articulating a voiceless as opposed to a voiced stop. In the production of, say, *p*, the lips need to be tightly closed since the egressive pulmonic air comes to the oral cavity unimpeded by the vocal bands (they are open), therefore great stricture is required to occlude the air stream. In the articulation of a *b* the air is already partially impeded at the vocal bands thus the occluding force at the lips need not be so strong. A click, *ĩk̃*, for example, involves voicelessness, two points of articulation (both occlusive), and suction, and is stronger and more marked than a segment such a *p*.

5.5.1 The ideal distinctive feature inventory, as a phonetic theory of phonological systems, should reflect greater and greater strength with more and more positive specifications of segments thus providing more marks for marked segments and a positive correlation for segmental strength hierarchies such as Hooper's. To test both the strength hierarchy and distinctive feature hypotheses one can compare the average numbers of positive distinctive feature specifications of segments included in the hierarchy with their intuitive arrangements in the hierarchy. To this end I have made an inventory of segments which purports to represent the distinctive human articulatory possibilities. While it does not exhaust the anthropophonic potential (probably a half million sounds), it represents a reasonably thorough sampling from which reliable averages of positive specifications can be acquired to represent the relative strength of the segment types in the hierarchy. The segments are:

Representative Anthropophonic Inventory

Occlusives (96)

Voiceless (52)	p	t	ṭ	c	k	X	ʔ
aspirated	pʰ	tʰ	ṭʰ	cʰ	kʰ		
glottalic	p'	t'	ṭ'	c'	k'		

Representative Anthropophonic Inventory

click	$\widehat{pk}$	$\widehat{tk}$	$\widehat{\underline{t}k}$	$\widehat{ck}$	
affricate	pₚ	ts	$\underline{t}s$	c	k^x
aspir.	$pₚ^h$	ts^h	$\underline{t}s^h$	c^h	kx^h
glott.	pₚ'	ts'	$\underline{t}s'$	c'	kx'
lateral		$\widehat{tl}$	$\widehat{\underline{t}l}$	$\widehat{cl}$	
labialized	p^w	t^w	$\underline{t}^w$	c^w	k^w
tense	*p	*t̩	*$\underline{t}$	*c	*k
lat. click		$\widehat{tlk}$	$\widehat{\underline{t}lk}$	$\widehat{clk}$	

Occlusives

Voiced (44)	b	d	ḍ	j	g	G
aspirated	b^h	d^h	$ḍ^h$	j^h	g^h	
affricate	bₚ	dz	dz̩	j	gɡ	
lateral		$\widehat{dl}$	$\widehat{ḍl}$	$\widehat{jl}$		
labial	b^w	d^w	$ḍ^w$	j^w	g^w	
ingressive	ɓ	ɗ	ɗ̣	ʄ	ɠ	
nasal	bm	dn	ḍṇ	jñ	gn	
	bmb	dnd	ḍṇḍ	jñj	gng	
	mb	nd	ṇḍ	ñj	ng	

Fricatives (24)

Voiceless (13)

slit	f	θ	ꝑ̥	ꝑ̥	$\underset{\smile}{x}$	x	ꭓ̵
groove	₽		s	ṣ	š		
lateral			ł̥				

Voiced

slit	v	đ	ꝑ	ꝑ̣	ǥ̰	ɡ	ɢ̵
groove	ƀ		z	ẓ	ž		
lateral			ł				

Liquids (20)

Voiced (10) (+Voiceless 20)

nasal	m	n	ñ	ŋ	
lateral		l	ʎ	ⱡ	
vibrant		r	r̃	R	

Vocoids (19) (+Voiceless, 38)

i		ü			ï	U	u	
	I			ɨ	i̇			
e		ö		ə	ɹ	ë	ɏ̈	o
	ɛ̧	ǫ̈				ɏ̧		ʻ
	ae					ᴀ		

5.5.2.1 In order to test the way in which distinctive feature inventories reflect the strength of segments, I devised matrices (see Appendix B) in which I specified the segments in the inventory above first using the SPE feature inventory which consists of the following primes:

SPE Distinctive Features

1. sonorant	11. lateral	20. primary d.r.
2. vocalic	12. high	21. secondary d.r.
3. consonantal	13. low	22. pressure
4. coronal	14. back	23. velaric
5. anterior	15. voice	24. glottalic
6. round	16. strident	25. tension
7. distributed	17. continuant	26. length
8. covered	18. suction	27. pitch
9. nasal	19. high sub	28. stress[6]
10. glot constr.	glot. pressure	

Counting and averaging the positive specifications in the matrices yielded the following results, in the order of descending positive specifications:

SPE Phonetic Strength Hierarchy

Segment Type	Average +'s	Hooper's Value
Liquids	7.33 ~ 7.83*	2
Voiceless Fric.	7.18	5
Voiced Fric.	6.75	4
Nasals	6 ~ 6.5*	3
Voiced Stops	5.93	5
Voiceless Stops	5.88	6
Vocoids	5.55 ~ 6*	0
Glides	5.5	1

*Average number of +'s counting only voiced segments.

5.5.2.2 The hierarchy established by counting the average number of positive specifications of all segments is unsatisfactory, but it becomes even more so if one counts only the natural, i.e., voiced, liquids and nasals. It is small wonder that linguists trying to establish strength hierarchies, but committed to using SPE features, had to claim that strength was not a phonetic concept. One can, of course, argue that the SPE features were not designed to reflect the strength of segments, but, then, one must ask, what was their purpose? If an alternate set, with fewer primes, can distinguish all the segments the SPE set distinguishes, and can be used to write rules in an economic fashion, then it is a better theory. If it also reflects the strength of segments in a manner consistent with that which linguists have felt to be correct, then it is even better. The revised set of articulatory primes accomplishes both missions.

Revised Distinctive Features

1. contoid	8. palatal	15. widened glottis
2. nasal	9. occlusion	16. constricted
3. surd	10. friction	glottis
4. labial	11. slit	17. suction
5. high	12. lateral	18. velaric
6. raised	13. delay. trans. 1	19. glottalic
7. dorsal	14. delay. trans. 2	

The following table shows the average number of positive specifications in the matrices using the revised inventory of distinctive features.

Revised DF Strength Hierarchy—Hooper's

Segment Type	Average +'s		Hooper's Value
Voiceless Occ.	6.52		6
Voiced Occ.	5.23		5
Voiceless Fric.	5.08		5
Voiced Fric.	4.08		4
Nasals	4.5	4*	3
Liquids	4.08	3.5*	2
Glides (y, w)	3.5		1
Vocoids	3.18	2.68*	0

*Average number of +'s counting only voiced segments.

5.6 In Chapter IV, I compared and contrasted the distinctive features proposed by JFH with those proposed here. I found that seven of the features are the rough equivalents of one another, that [lateral] is an apt substitute for [vocalic] and that one more articulation parameter [nondiffuse] must be added as well as a friction parameter. Adding these parameters, replacing [voiced] with [surd], [tense] with [widened glottis] (see 3.2.3.1–4) and adding the prosodic features make the inventory proposed here and the JFH inventory rough equivalents— the only difference is in the point of articulation features [labial, high, raised, dorsal] which contrast with [compact, nondiffuse, grave, flat]. The revised JFH inventory contains the following primes:

1. consonantal	6. grave	11. lateral	16. slit
2. nasal	7. flat	12. DT 1°	17. suction
3. surd	8. sharp	13. DT 2°	18. velaric
4. compact	9. interrupted	14. wide glot.	19. glottalic
5. nondiffuse	10. friction	15. checked	

Strength Hierarchy—Revised JFH D.F.'s[7]

Segment Types	Average +'s	Hooper's Value
Voiceless Occ.	5.52	6
Voiceless Fric.	4.41	5
Voiced Occl.	4.34	5
Voiced Fric.	3.42	4
Nasals (voiced)	3.25	3
Liquids (voiced)	2.33	2
Vocoids	2.21	1 – 0

The revised JFH specifications reconfirm the strength hierarchy as set forth by Hooper. Had [voiced] and [tense] been maintained as primes, along with [vocalic] and [strident], this would not have been the case. The classification that the parameters [compact, nondiffuse, grave, and flat] provide for vocoids: high – 1.7, mid – 2.6, and low – 2 run against the belief that the higher the vocoid the higher the strength. For the time being then, I submit that the feature system that I propose is the best of the three in existence since it distinguishes all that the SPE set does but uses fewer primes; it is of higher observational adequacy than the PSA primes; and it reflects the strength of segments better than the official version of either of the opposing theories.

5.7 The distinctive feature inventory that I propose is motivated on phonetic, phonological, and semiotic grounds rather than as an attempt to reflect the strength hierarchy that linguists have believed in. Its reflection of this hierarchy gives the inventory added credibility and buttresses the hierarchy which up to now has been based on linguists' intuitions rather than on theoretical primes. Future research in syllable structure, dynamic phonology (metasteses), phonological evolution, segmental relative frequency in texts, and markedness will serve as tests of descriptive and explanatory adequacy of these primes as a theory of phonological systems. I hope that the five chapters of this monograph plus the information in Appendices A and B will motivate phonologists to take these primes seriously and to reëxamine problematic areas of segmental description using them as analytic primes. I have used them in studies I have already published (1979,

1980a) and have found that they work quite well. I must admit, however, that much more rigorous testing is necessary before they can be accepted as the distinctive phonetic primes of phonological analysis.

Footnotes

[1] An earlier version of this chapter is Brakel (1979). I am grateful to the Chicago Linguistic Society for allowing me to publish this version.

[2] Foley takes no stand on the relative strength of palatal and pharyngeal segments.

[3] Foley does not include voiceless fricatives in this sub-hierarchy.

[4] Foley considers the propensity to vocalize a strength. Vocalization, to be in line with primes 1 and 2, should be seen as a weakening and *r* should, perhaps, be given the lowest number and *t*, the highest.

[5] Foley considers *p* a tightly bound *kw*.

[6] Pitch and stress are not considered in segmental specification. They are included here because they are part of the SPE inventory.

[7] The matrices for all these tables can be found in Appendix B.

Appendix A
The Specificatory Adequacy of the Revised Distinctive Features

A.1 Chapter III examines the SPE distintive features in detail and demonstrates their relative inadequacy as phonetic primes for phonological description. It excises counter-productive or inadequate primes and proposes a more elegant set. Before asking readers to accept this set, notwithstanding Chapters IV and V, I should also demonstrate their capability to distinguish segments in a wide range of phonological systems and their non-universal nature (the fact that no feature is necessary in every phonological system of the world). To these ends I have specified the phonemes of 23 different languages which I selected from the 700 illustrated in Ruhlen (1976). I chose these languages because their phoneme inventories contain unusual segments, many segments, or remarkably few segments, and because these languages are, for the most part, relatively unrelated. In all cases, the primes were adequate for specifying all of the segments.

A.2 The following table contrasts the complexity of the systems under study in three dimensions: the number of contrastive segments in each system, the average number of positive specifications per segment, and the number of distinctive features necessary to specify all the segments in each system so that they stand in contrast.

A.3 Because of the unusual nature of these systems and the limited sample, 23 out of 700, these averages probably do not represent the averages one would get by specifying all the systems known in the world. There is, in addition, no guarantee that the inventories of phonemes were achieved by uniform principles since many different researchers representing many different schools of linguistic description were involved in making these analyses (see especially the section on Lapp). To a degree, then, these figures and the inventories are suspect. Nonetheless, these inventories help test the observational adequacy of the revised features since their segments have been postulated and identified by linguists.

67

Hierarchical Arrangement of Phonological
Complexity

# of Segments		# Pos. Specs.		# D.F.'s	
1. Kung	116	1. Kung	6.53	1. Kung	19
2. Lapp	102	2. Abkhazian	5.35	2. !ko	17
3. Urdu	80	3. !ko	5.17	3. Gbeya	17
4. !ko	72	4. Lapp	4.79	4. Abkhazian	15
5. Eg. Arab	64	5. Chipewyan	4.65	5. Chipewyan	15
6. Abkhazian	60	6. Amharic	4.64	6. Amharic	15
7. Amharic	59	7. Urdu	4.55	7. Lapp	14
8. Chipewyan	57	8. Daju	4.25	8. Urdu	14
9. Gbeya	52	9. Buang	4.06	9. Koalib	14
10. Daju	51	10. Eg. Arab	4.02	10. Afrikaans	14
11. Norwegian	41	11. Afrikaans	4.00	11. Eg. Arab	13
12. Afrikaans	38	12. Gbeya	3.94	12. Bini	14
13. Koalib	37	13. Koalib	3.70	13. Daju	13
14. Bini	36	14. Bini	3.47	14. Norwegian	13
15. Buang	30	15. Norwegian	3.44	15. Buang	12
16. Nunggubuyu	22	16. Nunggubuyu	3.27	16. Alabaman	10
17. Alabaman	20	17. Dyirbal	3.25	17. Nunggubuyu	10
18. Andoa	18	18. Alabaman	2.70	18. Andoa	8
19. Aleut	18	19. Cherokee	2.56	19. Cherokee	8
20. Cherokee	16	20. Gadsup	2.33	20. Dyirbal	8
21. Dyirbal	16	21. Aleut	2.28	21. Gadsup	7
22. Gadsup	15	22. Andoa	2.11	22. Aleut	7
23. Mura	11	23. Mura	2.09	23. Mura	6
TOTALS	1031		87.15		283

Average # of Seg. 44.83   Average # Pos. Spec. 3.79   Average # D.F.'s 12.30

ABKHAZIAN

The phonemic inventory used in this study appears in Ruhlen (153):

ABKHAZIAN (Abzhui) [Lomtatidze 1967a] [Caucasian: North:
Northwest]
[SW USSR (Abxaz SSR); 90,000]

p^h $p^ʔ$ $t^h_{\wedge}$ $t^ʔ_{\wedge}$ $t^{hw}_{\wedge}$ $t^{ʔw}_{\wedge}$ k^h $k^ʔ$ k^{hj} $k^{ʔj}$ K^{hw} $k^{ʔw}$ $q^ʔ$ $q^{ʔj}$ $q^{ʔw}$ $ɨ$ j w

b $d_{\wedge}$ $d^w_{\wedge}$ g g^j g^w a

$t^{sh}_{\wedge}$ $t^{sʔ}_{\wedge}$ $t^{shw}_{\wedge}$ $t^{sʔ}_{\wedge}w$ $č^h$ $č^ʔ$ $č^{hj}$ $č^{ʔj}$ $[\bar{a}]$

$d^z_{\wedge}$ $d^{zw}_{\wedge}$ $ʝ$ $ʝ^j$

f $s_{\wedge}$ $š$ $š^j$ $š_w$ x x^j x^w h h^w SOV/AN

v $z_{\wedge}$ $ž$ $ž^j$ $ž^w$ $ɣ$ $ɣ^j$ $ɣ^ω$ $ɦ$

m $n_{\wedge}$

      l

      r

Remarkable here is the extremely elaborate consonantal inventory with only two vowels. The contoid inventory contains dental contoids [t̪ʰ], etc. which receive the following specification:

$$\begin{bmatrix} +\text{contoid} \\ -\text{labial} \\ -\text{raised} \\ \pm\text{occlusion} \\ \pm\text{friction} \end{bmatrix}$$

The distinctive features in use here allow us to distinguish dental contoids from alveolars without invoking a feature such as SPE [distributed]; [raised] indicates an articulatory gesture in which the tongue front goes higher than the teeth in contoidal articulation. The uvular stops, /q̊ʔ/ etc. are considered [+raised] since the back is raised but [–high] since the uvula descends to make the articulation. Using [raised] as defined here we can distinguish between both dental and alveolar contoids as well as uvular and velar articulation.

Abkhazian contoids also stand in contrast according to their palatal, and labial timbres which are indicated by the addition of these features to the specifications:

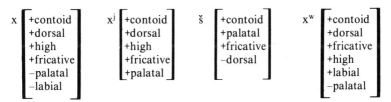

$$x \begin{bmatrix} +\text{contoid} \\ +\text{dorsal} \\ +\text{high} \\ +\text{fricative} \\ -\text{palatal} \\ -\text{labial} \end{bmatrix} \quad x^{j} \begin{bmatrix} +\text{contoid} \\ +\text{dorsal} \\ +\text{high} \\ +\text{fricative} \\ +\text{palatal} \end{bmatrix} \quad š \begin{bmatrix} +\text{contoid} \\ +\text{palatal} \\ +\text{fricative} \\ -\text{dorsal} \end{bmatrix} \quad x^{w} \begin{bmatrix} +\text{contoid} \\ +\text{dorsal} \\ +\text{fricative} \\ +\text{high} \\ +\text{labial} \\ -\text{palatal} \end{bmatrix}$$

In the case of palatalized palatal contoids, /šʲ, žʲ, čʰʲ/ etc, they are marked twice for [palatal] to distinguish them from their closest congeners (cf. section on Lapp).

The most complex segment of this complex inventory is /čʼʲ/, a palatalized palatal glottalic affricate which needs 11 positive specifications to be identified and to contrast with /čʰʲ/.

Abkhazian 1

PRIMES	pʰ	p?	tʰ	t?	tʰʷ	tʷ	kʰ	k?	kʰʷ	k?ʷ	kʰʲ	q?	q?ʲ	q?ʷ	b	d	dʷ	g	gʲ	gʷ	tsʰ	ts?	tsʷ	tsʲ	čʰ	č?	čʰʲ	č?ʲ	dz
contoid	+	+	+	+	+	+	+	+	+	+	+	+	+	+	+	+	+	+	+	+	+	+	+	+	+	+	+	+	+
nasal																													
surd	+	+	+	+	+	+	+	+	+	+	+	+	+	+							+	+	+	+	+	+	+	+	
labial	+	+			+	+			+	+				+	+		+			+			+						
high							+	+	+	+	+							+	+	+							+	+	
raised							+	+	+	+	+	+	+	+				+	+	+					+	+	+	+	
dorsal							+	+	+	+	+	+	+	+				+	+	+					+	+	+	+	
palatal											+		+						+					+	+	+	+	+	
occlusion	+	+	+	+	+	+	+	+	+	+	+	+	+	+	+	+	+	+	+	+	+	+	+	+	+	+	+	+	+
friction																					+	+	+	+	+	+	+	+	+
slit																													
lateral																													
DT 1°																					+	+	+	+	+	+	+	+	+
DT 2°																													
Wide Glot	+		+		+		+		+		+										+		+		+		+		
Glot. Const.																													
suction																													
velaric																													
glottalic		+		+		+		+		+		+	+	+								+		+		+		+	
Positive Specs.	5	5	4	4	5	4	7	7	8	8	8	6	7	7	3	2	3	5	6	6	6	6	6	6	9	9	10	10	4

Abkhazian - 2

PRIMES	dz	ǯ	ǯʲ	f	s	š	šʲ	šʷ	xʲ	xʷ	h	hʷ	v	z	ž	žʲ	žʷ	ɣ	ɣʲ	ɣʷ	ɦ	m	n	l	r	i	a	j	w
contoid	+	+	+	+	+	+	+	+	+	+			+	+	+	+	+	+	+	+		+	+	+	+				
nasal																						+	+						
surd				+	+	+	+	+	+	+	+	+																	
labial	+			+				+		+		+	+				+			+		+							+
high		+	+			+	+	+	+	+					+	+	+	+	+	+						+		+	+
raised		+	+			+	+	+	+	+					+	+	+	+	+	+						+		+	+
dorsal		+	+			+	+	+	+	+					+	+	+	+	+	+				+	+				+
palatal			+				+		+							+			+							+		+	
occlusion	+	+	+																										
friction	+	+	+	+	+	+	+	+	+	+	+	+	+	+	+	+	+	+	+	+	+								
slit									+	+																			
lateral																								+					
DT 1°	+	+	+																										
DT 2°																													
Wide Glot																												+	+
Glot. Const.																													
suction																													
velaric																													
glottalic																													
Positive Specs.	5	7	8	4	3	6	7	7	8	8	2	3	3	2	5	6	6	5	6	6	1	3	2	3	2	3	0	4	5

AFRIKAANS

The phonemic inventory of Afrikaans possesses a vowel system that is more elaborate than most examined here, yet neither the vowel system nor the four distinctive points of articulation of the contoids pose a problem for the features proposed here. The system:

AFRIKAANS [Pienaar and Hooper 1948] [Indo-European: Germanic: West]
[South Africa; 2.5 million]

```
p   t   c   k              i   y   u      ī   ȳ        ū
b   d     g                      ɔ   o    ɩ   ȳᵛ       ə̄
      č̌                    ɛ   œ    ɔ              [ə̄]
f   s   š   [ç]  x               a        ε̄        ɔ̄
v         ɟ̂ᶺ   ɦ                                    ɒ̄
m   n  [ɲ]  ŋ
    l
    r
```

approaches the mean in the number of phonemes, in the average number of positive specifications per phoneme, and in the number of distinctive features needed to specify all the contrasting segments:

AFRIKAANS - 1

PRIMES	p	t	c	k	b	d	g	č	f	s	š	x	v	j	ɦ	m	n	ŋ	l	r	i	y	ę	œ	ə	a	ɔ	o	u	ī
contoid	+	+	+	+	+	+	+	+	+	+	+	+	+	+		+	+	+	+	+										
nasal																+	+	+												
surd	+	+	+	+					+	+	+	+	+																	
labial	+				+					+			+			+						+		+			+	+	+	
high			+	+			+	+			+	+		+				+			+	+							+	+
raised		+	+	+		+	+	+		+	+	+		+			+	+	+	+	+	+	+	+		+	+	+	+	+
dorsal			+				+					+						+									+	+	+	
palatal			+								+			+							+	+	+	+						+
occlusion	+	+	+	+	+	+	+	+						+																
friction									+	+	+	+	+	+	+															
slit									+			+	+																	
lateral																			+											
DT 1°									+				+																	+
DT 2°																												+		
Wide Glot																														
Glot. Const.																														
suction																														
velaric																														
glottalic																														
Positive Specs.	4	4	6	6	3	3	5	8	5	4	6	7	4	7	1	3	3	5	3	2	3	4	2	3	1	0	4	3	4	4

AFRIKAANS - 2

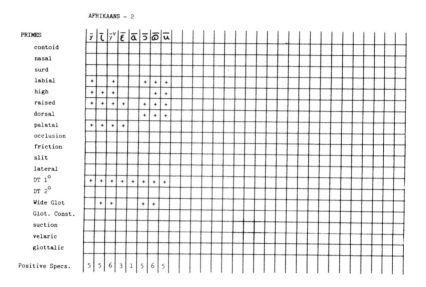

PRIMES	ȳ	ι	ȳᵛ	ε̄	ā	ɔ	ō̄	ū
contoid								
nasal								
surd								
labial	+		+		+	+	+	
high	+	+	+			+	+	
raised	+	+	+	+		+	+	+
dorsal					+	+	+	
palatal	+	+	+	+				
occlusion								
friction								
slit								
lateral								
DT 1°	+	+	+	+	+	+	+	+
DT 2°								
Wide Glot		+	+		+	+		
Glot. Const.								
suction								
velaric								
glottalic								
Positive Specs.	5	5	6	3	1	5	6	5

ALABAMAN

This inventory

ALABAMAN [Rand 1968] [Macro-Algonquian: Muskogean] [Texas; 400]

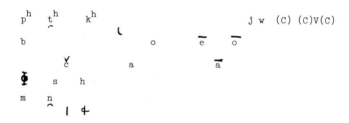

presents no problem for the features proposed here. It is included because it contains relatively few segments, because the feature [high] is not necessary.

ALABAMAN

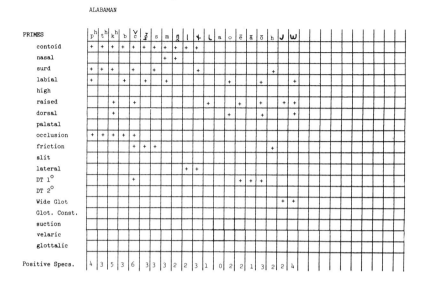

PRIMES	pʰ	tʰ	kʰ	b	č	ǰ	s	m	ṇ	l	ɬ	ʟ	a	o	ē	ā	ō	h	J	W
contoid	+	+	+	+	+	+	+	+	+	+	+									
nasal								+	+											
surd	+	+	+		+		+				+							+		
labial	+			+				+						+			+			+
high			+																	+
raised					+	+									+				+	+
dorsal			+											+			+			+
palatal																				
occlusion	+	+	+	+	+															
friction					+	+	+													
slit																				
lateral										+	+	+								
DT 1°					+										+	+	+			
DT 2°																				
Wide Glot																		+	+	
Glot. Const.																				
suction																				
velaric																				
glottalic																				
Positive Specs.	4	3	5	3	6	3	3	3	2	2	3	1	0	2	2	1	3	2	2	4

Aleut

Beyond the sparseness of segments in this inventory,

ALEUT (Eastern) [Geoghegan 1944] [Eskimo-Aleut: Aleut] [Alaska (Aleutian Islands); 600]

it is remarkable because there is no need for the feature [contoid] since there is no /r/ phoneme which would be negatively specified for all exclusively contoidal articulatory gestures and, thus, possibly confused with vocoid.

ALEUT

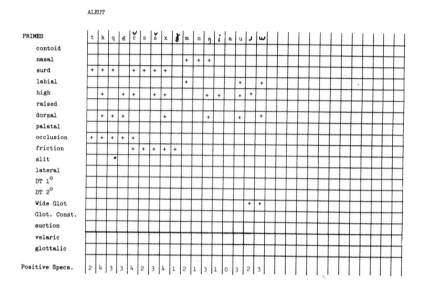

PRIMES	t	k	q	g	č	s	š	x	ǰ	m	n	ŋ	i	a	u	J	w									
contoid																									
nasal										+	+	+													
surd	+	+	+		+	+	+	+																	
labial								+							+	+									
high		+		+	+		+	+			+	+	+		+	+									
raised																									
dorsal		+	+	+				+				+			+	+									
palatal																									
occlusion	+	+	+	+	+																				
friction						+	+	+	+	+															
slit		•																							
lateral																									
DT 1°																									
DT 2°																									
Wide Glot														+	+										
Glot. Const.																									
suction																									
velaric																									
glottalic																									
Positive Specs.	2	4	3	3	4	2	3	4	1	2	1	3	1	0	3	2	3								

AMHARIC

This inventory is included

AMHARIC (Addis Ababa) [Leslau 1968] [Afro-Asiatic: Semitic: South: Ethiopic] [Ethiopia; 8 million]   SOV/AN

```
p  p̄  pʼ  p̄ʼ     t  t̄  tʼ  t̄ʼ              k  k̄  kʼ  k̄ʼ  kʷ  kʷʼ  [ʔ]  i  ɨ  u  j  w
b  b̄              d  d̄                       g  ḡ  gʷ                            e  ə  o
                     č  č̄  čʼ   č̄ʼ                                                a
                     ǰ  ǰ̄
f  f̄              s  s̄  sʼ s̄ʼ š̄  š̄                h  hʷ
                     z
m  m̄              n  n̄              ɲ  ɲ̄
                     l  l̄
                     r  r̄
```

because of its relative complexity and because of its utilization of the glottalic air stream in contoidal articulation. I find it remarkable that this language systematically distinguishes between long and non-long glottalic contoids.

Appendix A

AMHARIC

PRIMES	p	p̄	p'	p̄'	t	t̄	t'	t̄'	k	k̄	k'	k̄'	kʷ	kʷ'	b	ḏ	d̄	g	ḡ	gʷ	č	č̥	č'	č̄'	ǰ	ǰ̄	f	f̄	s	
contoid	+	+	+	+	+	+	+	+	+	+	+	+	+	+	+	+	+	+	+	+	+	+	+	+	+	+	+	+	+	
nasal																														
surd	+	+	+	+	+	+	+	+	+	+	+	+	+								+	+	+	+			+	+	+	
labial	+	+	+	+									+	+	+	+			+								+	+		
high									+	+	+	+	+	+				+	+	+	+	+	+	+	+	+				
raised									+	+	+	+	+	+				+	+	+	+	+	+	+	+	+				
dorsal									+	+	+	+	+	+				+	+	+										
palatal																					+	+	+	+	+	+				
occlusion	+	+	+	+	+	+	+	+	+	+	+	+	+	+	+	+	+	+	+	+	+	+	+	+	+	+				
friction																					+	+	+	+	+	+	+	+	+	
slit																														
lateral																														
DT 1°		+		+		+		+		+		+				+		+		+		+	+	+	+	+	+		+	
DT 2°																					+		+		+					
Wide Glot																														
Glot. Const.																														
suction																														
velaric																														
glottalic		+	+			+	+			+	+		+									+	+							
Positive Specs.	4	5	5	6	3	4	4	5	6	7	7	8	7	8	3	4	2	3	5	6	6	8	9	9	10	7	8	4	5	3

AMHARIC - 2

PRIMES	s̱	ŝ	ŝ'	s̄̌	š̌	h	hʷ	z	ž	z̄̌	m	m̄	n	n̄	ŋ	ū	l	l̄	ç	r	i	e	*	ə	a	o	u	J	ɯ
contoid	+	+	+	+	+			+	+	+	+	+	+	+	+	+	+	+	+	+									
nasal											+	+	+	+	+	+													
surd	+	+	+	+	+	+	+																						
labial							+				+	+														+	+		+
high			+	+				+	+				+	+					+		+					+	+	+	+
raised			+	+				+	+				+	+		+	+	+	+	+	+					+	+		+
dorsal													+	+												+	+		+
palatal			+	+				+	+										+	+							+		
occlusion																													
friction	+	+	+	+	+	+	+	+	+	+																			
slit																													
lateral																	+	+											
DT 1°		+		+					+		+		+		+		+		+										
DT 2°																													
Wide Glot																												+	+
Glot. Const.																													
suction																													
velaric																													
glottalic		+	+																										
Positive Specs.		4	4	5	6	7	2	3	2	5	6	3	4	2	3	5	6	2	3	2	3	3	2	2	1	0	3	4	4	5

ANDOA

This inventory

ANDOA (Iquito) [Eastman and Eastman 1963] [Andean-Equatorial: Andean: Zaparoan] [N Peru; 500]

p	t	k	[ʔ]	i	ɨ	u	ī̃	ɨ̃	ū̃	j	w	high tone
	s	.		h̃		a		ã				(c) (c)v
m	n											SVO/AN
	r											

is included because of its segmental sparseness and because of the unusual segment, /h̃/, a surd, non-contoidal, nasalized fricative.

ANDOA

PRIMES	p	t	k	s	·m	n	r	i	ɨ	a	u	ī̃	ɨ̃	ã	ū̃	h	ɟ	ɯ
contoid	+	+	+	+	+	+	+											
nasal					+	+								+				
surd														+		+		
labial	+			+							+			+		+	+	
high			+					+	+		+	+	+		+		+	+
raised																		
dorsal																		
palatal						+				+								
occlusion																		
friction				+										+				
slit																		
lateral																		
DT 1°						+			+	+	+	+						
DT 2°																		
Wide Glot														+	+			
Glot. Const.																		
suction																		
velaric																		
glottalic																		
Positive Specs.	2	1	2	2	3	2	2	2	1	0	2	3	2	1	3	3	3	4

EGYPTIAN ARABIC

The inventory of Egyptian Arabic

(EGYPTIAN) ARABIC (Colloquial) [Mitchell 1962] [Afro-Asiatic: Semitic: South: Southwest] [Egypt; 45 million]

was included because of its pharyngeal segments /ħ, h̄, ʕ, ʕ̄/ which are specified as:

$$\begin{bmatrix} \text{+fricative} \\ \text{--glottal constriction} \\ \text{--contoid} \\ \pm\text{surd} \\ \pm\text{D.T.} \end{bmatrix}$$

These segments contrast with pharyngealized contoids /t^D, d^D, s^D, $š^D$/ etc. which have a pharyngeal timbre and are specified as follows:

$$\begin{bmatrix} \text{+contoid} \\ \text{+labial} \\ \text{+raised} \\ \left\{\begin{matrix}\pm\text{occlusion}\\ \pm\text{friction}\end{matrix}\right\} \\ \pm\text{surd} \end{bmatrix}$$

A phonological grammar of Arabic will state that raised contoids which have the feature [labial] will produce the extremity contraction at the pharynx.

ARABIC (Egyptian)

PRIMES	t̰	t̰ˀ	t̰̄	t̰ˀ̄	k	k̄	q	q̄	ʔ	ʔ̄	b	b̄	d̰	d̰̄	d̰ˀ	d̰ˀ̄	g	ḡ	f	f̄	s	s̄	š	š̄	ṣ	ṣ̄	ǧ	ǧ̄	x	x̄
contoid	+	+	+	+	+	+	+	+			+	+	+	+	+	+	+	+	+	+	+	+	+	+	+	+	+	+		
nasal																														
surd	+	+	+	+	+	+	+	+	+	+	+	+							+	+	+	+	+	+	+	+	+	+	+	+
labial		+		+							+	+					+	+		+		+							+	+
high					+	+											+	+					+	+						
raised	+	+	+	+	+	+	+	+					+	+	+	+	+	+			+	+	+	+	+	+	+	+		
dorsal					+	+	+	+									+	+									+	+		
palatal																									+	+				
occlusion	+	+	+	+	+	+	+	+	+	+	+	+	+	+	+	+	+	+												
friction																			+	+	+	+	+	+	+	+	+	+	+	+
slit																			+	+										
lateral																														
DT 1°		+	+		+		+		+		+		+		+		+				+	+			+		+		+	
DT 2°																														
Wide Glot																														
Glot. Const.									+	+																				
suction																														
velaric																														
glottalic																														
Positive Specs.	4	5	5	6	6	7	5	6	3	4	4	5	2	3	3	5	5	6	4	5	4	6	5	7	6	7	5	6	3	4

ARABIC (Egyptian) - 2

PRIMES	h	h̄	z	ẑ	z̄	ẑ̄	G	Ḡ	ʕ	ʕ̄	m	m̄	n	n̄	l	l̄	r	r̄	i̯	e	æ	ɔ	o	a	ū	ō	ā	ī	ē	ǣ
contoid			+	+	+	+	+	+			+	+	+	+	+	+	+	+												
nasal											+	+	+	+																
surd	+	+																												
labial				+		+			+	+	+	+									+	+		+	+					
high																	+				+			+			+			
raised			+	+	+	+	+	+							+	+	+	+	+	+			+	+	+	+	+	+		
dorsal					+	+															+	+		+	+					
palatal																	+	+	+									+	+	+
occlusion																														
friction	+	+	+	+	+	+	+	+	+	+																				
slit																														
lateral															+	+														
DT 1°		+			+	+		+		+		+		+		+								+	+	+	+	+	+	+
DT 2°																														
Wide Glot																														
Glot. Const.	+	+																												
suction																														
velaric																														
glottalic																														
Positive Specs.	3	4	3	4	4	5	4	5	2	3	3	4	2	3	3	4	2	3	3	2	1	4	3	0	5	4	1	4	3	2

ARABIC (Egyptian) - 3

PRIMES	J	J̄	w	w̄
contoid				
nasal				
surd				
labial			+	+
high	+	+	+	+
raised	+	+	+	+
dorsal			+	+
palatal	+	+		
occlusion				
friction				
slit				
lateral				
DT 1°		+		+
DT 2°				
Wide Glot	+	+	+	+
Glot. Const.				
suction				
velaric				
glottalic				
Positive Specs.	4	5	5	6

BINI

This inventory

BINI [Wescott 1965] [Niger-Kordofanian: Niger-Congo: Kwa: Edo] [W Nigeria; 300,000]

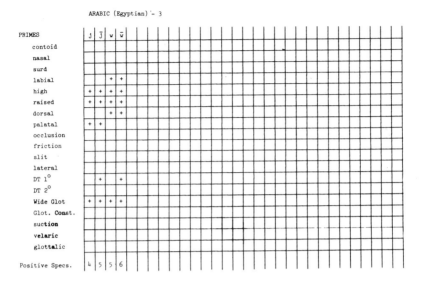

was included because of the coarticulated stops /k͡p, g͡b/. These segments, if specified as

$$\begin{bmatrix} +\text{contoid} \\ +\text{occlusion} \\ +\text{dorsal} \\ +\text{labial} \\ +\text{high} \end{bmatrix}$$

would not contrast with /kʷ/ and /gʷ/, labialized velars. Likewise they pose the problem of how one would specify theoretically possible labial contoids with velar timbres, i.e. *pˣ*, *bᵍ*. I propose the following:

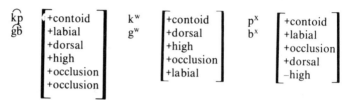

$$
\widehat{kp}\ \widehat{gb}\
\begin{bmatrix}
+\text{contoid}\\
+\text{labial}\\
+\text{dorsal}\\
+\text{high}\\
+\text{occlusion}\\
+\text{occlusion}
\end{bmatrix}
\qquad
k^{w}\ g^{w}\
\begin{bmatrix}
+\text{contoid}\\
+\text{dorsal}\\
+\text{high}\\
+\text{occlusion}\\
+\text{labial}
\end{bmatrix}
\qquad
p^{x}\ b^{x}\
\begin{bmatrix}
+\text{contoid}\\
+\text{labial}\\
+\text{occlusion}\\
+\text{dorsal}\\
-\text{high}
\end{bmatrix}
$$

This solution for such contrasts resembles those for palatalization and pharyngealization which distinguishes timbres from articulations. I consider it debatable whether or not to add a delayed transition feature to the specification of coarticulated stops. For the time being and the purposes of this exposition, their special status is recognized by two positive specifications for [occlusion].

BINI

PRIMES	p	t	k	k͡p	b	d	g	g͡b	f	s	x	β	v	z	ɣ	m	n	l	ļ	r	ɼ	h	i	e	ɛ	a	ɔ	o	u	ĩ
contoid	+	+	+	+	+	+	+	+	+	+	+	+	+	+	+	+	+	+	+	+	+	+								
nasal																+	+													+
surd	+	+	+	+					+	+	+								+		+	+								
labial	+			+	+			+	+			+	+			+											+	+	+	
high			+	+			+	+			+				+								+						+	+
raised			+	+			+	+			+				+				+	+	+		+	+	+		+	+	+	+
dorsal			+	+			+	+			+				+												+			
palatal																														
occlusion	+	+	+	++	+	+	+	++																						
friction									+	+	+	+	+	+	+															
slit									+		+		+		+															
lateral																		+	+											
DT 1°																														
DT 2°																														
Wide Glot																									+		+			
Glot. Const.																														
suction																														
velaric																														
glottalic																														
Positive Specs.	4	3	6	8	3	2	5	7	5	3	7	3	4	2	6	3	2	2	4	2	3	2	2	1	2	0	4	2	3	3

BINI - 2

PRIMES	$\widetilde{\xi}$	$\widetilde{\alpha}$	$\mathcal{S}$	$\mathcal{T}$	ɟ	w																																				
contoid																																											
nasal	+	+	+	+																																							
surd																																											
labial			+	+		+																																					
high			+	+	+																																						
raised	+		+	+	+	+																																					
dorsal			+	+		+																																					
palatal																																											
occlusion																																											
friction																																											
slit																																											
lateral																																											
DT 1°																																											
DT 2°																																											
Wide Glot	+		+		+	+																																					
Glot. Const.																																											
suction																																											
velaric																																											
glottalic																																											
Positive Specs.	3	1	5	5	3	5																																					

BUANG

This inventory

BUANG (Central) [Hooley 1964] [Austro-Tai: Austronesian: Oceanic: Northeast New Guinea] [Territory of New Guinea (Morobe); 7,000]

p   t   k k^W q   ˙i   u   j   w
^{m}b ^{n}d   ꝡg   ꝡg^W ᴺꝺ   e   ɔ   o
             ꭚ   a

v   s   ꝩ   ꝗ
m   n   ꝺ   ꝺ$^\omega$ ᴎ
       l
       ꞔ

was included because of its uvular contoidal series and its prenasalized segments.

BUANG

PRIMES	p	t	k	kʷ	q	ᵐb	ⁿd	ⁿg	ᵑgʷ	ᵑɢ	ʝ	v	s	ɣ	ʁ	m	n	ŋ	ŋʷ	ɴ	l	r	i	e	ə	a	o	u	j	w
contoid	+	+	+	+	+	+	+	+	+	+	+	+	+	+	+	+	+	+	+	+	+	+								
nasal						+	+	+	+	+						+	+	+	+	+										
surd	+	+	+	+	+								+																	
labial	+			+		+			+			+				+			+								+	+		+
high			+	+				+	+		+			+				+	+				+					+	+	+
raised		+	+	+	+		+	+	+	+	+		+	+	+		+	+	+	+	+	+	+	+	+		+	+	+	+
dorsal			+	+	+			+	+	+				+	+			+	+								+	+		+
palatal											+												+	+					+	
occlusion	+	+	+	+	+	+	+	+	+	+	+																			
friction											+	+	+	+	+															
slit																														
lateral																					+									
DT 1°											+																			
DT 2°																														
Wide Glot																													+	+
Glot. Const.																														
suction																														
velaric																														
glottalic																														
Positive Specs.	4	4	6	7	5	4	4	6	7	5	7	3	4	5	4	3	3	5	6	3	3	2	3	2	1	0	3	4	4	5

CHEROKEE

This inventory

CHEROKEE [Bender and Harris 1946] [Macro-Siouan: Iroquoian: Southern]
[W North Carolina; 10,000]

```
        d̮     g     i     u     j   w
        s     h     e   ə   o
        z           a
  m     n̮
        l
```

was included because of its sparseness and because of the fact that, owing to its peculiar nature, [occlusion] is not a needed feature.

CHEROKEE

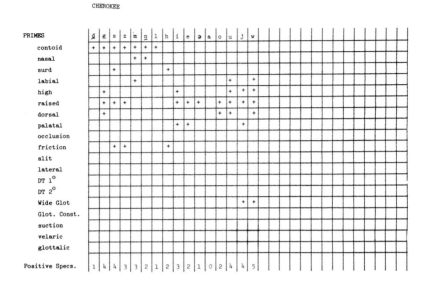

PRIMES	ǰ	g	s	z	m	ṇ	l	h	i	e	ə	a	o	u	ɟ	w
contoid	+	+	+	+	+	+	+									
nasal					+	+										
surd			+					+								
labial					+								+	+		+
high		+							+					+	+	+
raised		+	+	+					+	+	+			+	+	
dorsal		+											+	+		+
palatal									+	+					+	
occlusion																
friction			+	+				+								
slit																
lateral																
DT 1°																
DT 2°																
Wide Glot															+	+
Glot. Const.																
suction																
velaric																
glottalic																
Positive Specs.	1	4	4	3	3	2	1	2	3	2	1	0	2	4	4	5

CHIPEWYAN

This inventory

CHIPEWYAN (Fort Chipewyan) [Fang-Kuei 1946] [Na-Dene: Athapaskan-Eyak: Athapaskan] [Canada (Alberta); 5,000]

```
p     t   tʰ  t?              k  kʷ  kʰ  kʰʷ  k?  k?ʷ      ?          i   u   ī   ū   ĩ   ũ   ĩ̄   ū̃   j
 tθ  tθ̂h  tθ̂?  tŝ  tsh  tŝ?  tˡ  tˡh  tˡ?        cʕ  cʕh  cʕ?         e   o        ɛ̄       ɛ̃       ɛ̃̄
 θ   ṣ                        ʕ               x   xʷ   h                              ɛ
 ð   z                                        ɣ   ɣʷ                  a   ā   ã   ā̃
 m   ṇ
     l   ɬ
     r                                    SOV/NA              high
                                                              low
```

was included because of its complexity and because of its unusual segments: /tθ/, /cᶜ/, /tˡ/ etc., that is [+slit] affricates which contrast with /tˢ/ which are [−slit] and [−raised] i.e. dental, thus [−distributed] in the SPE features. This contrast, /tθ ~ tˢ/. cannot be made in the SPE features whereas it is easily made using the revised inventory. The lateral affricates are also unusual, but easily specified here.

CHIPEWYAN

PRIMES	p	t̂	tʰ	t?	k	kʷ	kʰ	kʰʷ	k?	k?ʷ	?	t̂ɵ	ɵʜ	ɵʔ	t̂s	sʜ	sʔ	t̂l	lʜ	lʔ	ĉ	ĉʜ	ĉʔ	ɵ	ʒ	ç	x	xʷ	h	?
contoid	+	+	+	+	+	+	+	+	+	+		+	+	+	+	+	+	+	+	+	+	+	+	+	+	+	+	+		+
nasal																														
surd	+	+	+	+	+	+	+	+	+	+	+	+	+	+	+	+	+	+	+	+	+	+	+	+	+	+	+	+		+
labial	+					+		+		+																		+		
high			+	+	+	+	+	+													+	+	+			+	+	+		
raised																+	+	+	+	+	+					+	+	+		
dorsal			+	+	+	+	+	+																		+	+			
palatal																					+	+	+							
occlusion	+	+	+	+	+	+	+	+	+	+	+	+	+	+	+	+	+	+	+	+	+	+	+							
friction												+	+	+	+	+	+	+	+	+	+	+	+	+	+	+	+	+	+	+
slit												+	+	+							+	+	+		+	+	+			+
lateral																		+	+	+										
DT 1°												+	+	+	+	+	+	+	+	+	+	+	+							
DT 2°																														
Wide Glot		+			+	+						+			+			+			+									
Glot. Const.									+																				+	
suction																														
velaric																														
glottalic		+				+	+						+			+			+			+								
Positive Specs.	4	3	4	4	5	6	6	7	6	7	3	6	7	7	5	6	6	7	8	8	9	10	10	4	3	6	7	8	3	3

CHIPEWAN - 2

PRIMES	z̧	ɣ	ɣʷ	m	ŋ	l	ɬ	r	i	e	a	o	u	ī	ē	ā	ō	ū	ĩ	ẽ	ã	ũ	ĩ	ẽ	ã	ũ	ɉ
contoid	+	+	+	+	+	+	+	+																			
nasal				+	+														+	+	+	+	+	+	+	+	
surd					+																						
labial		+	+							+	+		+	+			+	+		+			+				
high		+	+						+			+	+			+	+			+	+			+	+		
raised		+	+		+	+	+	+	+	+	+	+		+	+	+	+		+	+	+		+	+			
dorsal		+	+						+	+			+	+			+	+		+			+				
palatal				+	+					+	+				+	+				+	+			+			
occlusion																											
friction	+	+	+																								
slit																											
lateral					+	+																					
DT 1°												+	+	+	+	+					+	+	+	+			
DT 2°																											
Wide Glot																									+		
Glot. Const.																											
suction																											
velaric																											
glottalic																											
Positive Specs.	2	5	6	3	2	3	4	2	3	2	0	3	4	4	3	1	4	5	4	3	1	5	5	4	2	6	4

DAJU

This inventory

DAJU (Shatt) [Tucker and Bryan 1966] [Nilo-Saharan: Chari-Nile: Sudanic: Eastern] [W Sudan; 100,000]

was included because of its relative complexity and because of its unusal segments: prenasalized stops and fricatives, implosives and labialized contoids.

DAJU -2

PRIMES	ñ	n̄	ŋ	ŋ̄	ŋ̄ʷ	l	l̄	r	i	e	a	ɵ	o	u	ī	ē	ā	ɟ	ɟ̄	w	w̄
contoid	+	+	+	+	+	+	+	+													
nasal	+	+	+	+	+																
surd																					
labial					+							+	+	+						+	+
high	+	+	+	+	+				+					+	+			+	+	+	+
raised	+	+	+	+	+	+	+	+	+	+			+	+	+	+		+	+	+	+
dorsal			+	+	+							+	+						+	+	+
palatal	+	+							+	+					+	+		+	+		+
occlusion																					
friction																					
slit																					
lateral						+	+														
DT 1°		+		+			+											+	+	+	+
DT 2°																					
Wide Glot														+	+	+	+				
Glot. Const.																					
suction																					
velaric																					
glottalic																					
Positive Specs.	5	6	5	6	6	3	4	2	3	2	0	2	3	4	4	3	1	4	5	5	6

DYIRBAL

This inventory

DYRIBAL [Dixon 1972] [Australian: Pama-Nyungan: Pama-Maric:
Pama: Western] [NE Australia (N Queensland); 40]

```
b    d    ɟ    g       i    u    j    w    initial stress
m    n    ɲ    ŋ          a
     l                              SOV/NA
     r    ɳ
```

was included because of its simplicity and because of its lack of surds
proving that languages may exist with no voiceless segments whereas
no language exists which has no voiced segments. This supports my
assertion that [surd] is the marked quality.

DYIRBAL

PRIMES	b	d	ĵ	g	m	n	ñ	ŋ	l	r	ɟ	i	a	u	j	w
contoid	+	+	+	+	+	+	+	+	+	+	+					
nasal					+	+	+	+								
surd																
labial	+			+										+		+
high			+	+			+	+		+	+			+	+	+
raised		+		+	+	+	+	+	+		+	+		+	+	+
dorsal			+					+						+		+
palatal																
occlusion	+	+	+	+												
friction																
slit																
lateral									+							
DT 1°																
DT 2°																
Wide Glot															+	+
Glot. Const.																
suction																
velaric																
glottalic																
Positive Specs.	3	3	4	5	3	3	4	5	3	2	3	2	0	4	3	5

GADSUP

This inventory

GADSUP (Agarabi) [Goddard 1967] [Indo-Pacific: Central New Guinea: East New Guinea Highlands: Gauwa] [Territory of New Guinea (Eastern Highlands); 7,000]

```
p     t     k     ?       i     u      ε̄          j   w   SOV/AN
m           n                   e      ḁ̄
      ʃ
```

was included because of its simplicity and because, again, the feature [surd] is not a necessary ingredient, nor is [palatal] nor [high].

GADSUP

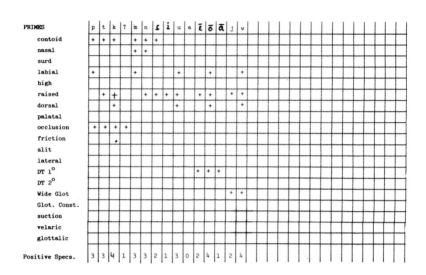

PRIMES	p	t	k	?	m	n	ꞇ	i	u	a	ɛ̄	ɔ̄	ā̃	j	w
contoid	+	+	+		+	+	+								
nasal					+	+									
surd															
labial	+				+				+			+			+
high															+
raised		+	+			+	+	+		+					+	+
dorsal			+						+			+		+	+
palatal															
occlusion	+	+	+	+											
friction				·											
slit															
lateral															
DT 1°											+	+	+		
DT 2°															
Wide Glot											+	+			
Glot. Const.															
suction															
velaric															
glottalic															
Positive Specs.	3	3	4	1	3	3	2	1	3	0	2	4	1	2	4

GBEYA

This inventory

GBEYA (Bossangoa) [Samarin 1966] [Niger-Kordofanian: Niger-Congo: Adamawa-Eastern: Eastern] [NW Central African Republic; 600,000]

```
p         t        k k͡p      ? i u    ī    ū    î̃    ũ̂    ĩ̄    ũ̃      j w
b  ᵐb     d ⁿd ɗ   g g͡b         e o    ē    ō
   ŋ g ᶮɟ͡ᵐ                       ɛ ɔ   ɛ̱̄    ɔ̱̄   æ ɑ   ɛ̱̄̃   ɑ̱̄̃       high
                                                                     low
f         s        h                                                 VH
v [ⱱ]     z
m ?m      n  ?ŋ    ŋ [ⱱ] IS A LABIODENTAL FLAP.
          l
          Ɬ
```

was included because of its complexity and because of its unusual segments: coarticulated velarolabials, /k͡p, g͡b, ŋ͡m/ (the nasal contoid is doubly marked for [nasal] as the occlusives are for [occlusion]); implosives, prenasalized stops, and preglottalized nasals, /ʔm, ʔn/. Glottalized segments are specified as contoids or vocoids plus [glottal constriction]. Preglottalized would be specified as e.g. ʔC [+contoid, +glottal constriction, +D.T.]. These are different from glottalic segments, Cʔ [±contoid] which use the glottalic air stream.

GBEYA

PRIMES	p	t	k	k͡p	ʔ	b	ᵐb	ɓ	d	ⁿd	ɗ	g	gb	ᵑg	ᵑᵐ	f	s	v	z	m	ᶠm	n	ʔn	ŋ	l	ʟ	i	e	ɛ	a
contoid	+	+	+	+	+	+	+	+	+	+	+	+	+	+	+	+	+	+	+	+	+	+	+	+	+	+				
nasal							+			+				++	+					+	+	+	+	+						
surd	+	+	+	+	+											+	+													
labial	+			+		+	+	+					+		+	+		+		+	+									
high			+	+								+	+	+	+										+		+	+		
raised		+	+	+					+	+	+	+	+	+			+		+			+	+	+	+	+		+	+	+
dorsal			+	+								+	+	+	+									+	+					+
palatal																											+	+	+	
occlusion	+	+	+	++		+	+	+	+	+	+	+	++	+	+															
friction																+	+	+	+											
slit																														
lateral																									+	+				
DT 1°																														
DT 2°																					+		+							
Wide Glot																														+
Glot. Const.																					+		+							
suction								+			+																			
velaric																														
glottalic																														
Positive Specs.	4	4	6	8	2	3	4	4	3	4	4	5	7	7	7	4	4	3	3	3	5	3	5	5	5	3	2	3	2	3

GBEYA - 2

PRIMES	ɔ	o	u	ī	ē	ɛ̄	ā	ū	ō	ɔ̄	ĩ	ɛ̃	ã	õ	ũ	ī̃	ɛ̃̄	ã̄	ȭ	ũ̄	J	w
contoid																						
nasal											+	+	+	+	+	+	+	+	+	+		
surd																						
labial	+	+	+					+	+	+				+	+				+	+		+
high		+	+					+			+				+	+				+	+	+
raised	+	+	+	+	+	+		+	+	+	+			+	+	+			+	+	+	+
dorsal	+	+	+					+	+					+	+				+	+		+
palatal				+	+	+					+	+				+	+				+	
occlusion																						
friction																						
slit																						
lateral																						
DT 1°				+	+	+	+	+	+	+						+	+	+	+	+		
DT 2°																						
Wide Glot	+					+				+									+	+		+
Glot. Const.																						
suction																						
velaric																						
glottalic																						
Positive Specs.	4	3	4	4	3	4	1	5	4	5	4	2	1	5	5	5	3	2	6	6	4	5

!KÕ

This inventory

!KO [Maingard 1958] [Khoisan: Southern] [NW Botswana]

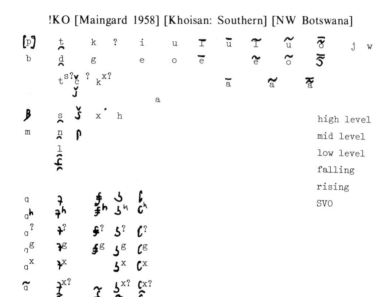

was included, along with that of Kung, because of the great number of segments and the especially elaborate set of clicks.

!KO −2

PRIMES	ʔ͓ˣ	ʔ͓ˣ̌	ʔ̂	ɟ	ɟ	ɟʰ	ɟʔ	ɟᵍ	ɟ̃	ɔ	ɔʰ	ɔʔ	ɔᵍ	ɔˣ	ɔˣʔ	ɔ̃	ʄ	ʄʰ	ʄʔ	ʄᵍ	ʄˣ	ʄˣʔ	ʄ̃	i	e	a	ɔ	o	u	ī	ē
contoid	+	+	+	+	+	+	+	+	+	+	+	+	+	+	+	+	+	+	+	+	+	+									
nasal		+					+							+							+										
surd	+	+	+	+	+		+	+	+	+		+	+	+	+	+	+	+		+	+	+									
labial																										+	+	+			
high													+	+	+	+	+	+	+	+								+	+		
raised			+	+	+	+	+	+	+	+	+	+	+	+	+	+	+	+	+	+	+	+		+	+			+	+	+	+
dorsal	+	+								+	+						+	+						+	+	+					
palatal																			+	+								+	+		
occlusion	+	+	+	+	+	+	+	+	+	+	+	+	+	+	+	+	+	+	+	+	+	+									
friction	+	+								+	+						+	+													
slit																															
lateral						+	+	+	+	+	+	+																			
DT 1°	+	+								+	+						+	+											+	+	
DT 2°																															
Wide Glot				+						+							+									+					
Glot. Const.																															
suction																															
velaric	+	+	+	+	+	+	+	+	+	+	+	+	+	+	+	+	+	+	+	+	+	+									
glottalic		+				+					+							+				+									
Positive Specs.	7	8	5	5	6	6	4	6	6	7	7	5	9	10	7	6	7	7	5	9	10	7	3	2	0	4	3	4	4	3	

!KO −3

PRIMES	ā	ū	ī͂	ē͂	ā͂	õ	ũ	ā̃	ō͂	ō͂	ɟ	w												
contoid																								
nasal			+	+	+	+	+	+	+															
surd																								
labial		+										+												
high		+	+			+			+	+														
raised		+	+	+		+	+	+	+															
dorsal		+			+	+	+	+		+														
palatal			+	+					+															
occlusion																								
friction																								
slit																								
lateral																								
DT 1°	+	+					+	+	+															
DT 2°																								
Wide Glot							+		+	+														
Glot. Const.																								
suction																								
velaric																								
glottalic																								
Positive Specs.	1	5	4	3	1	3	4	2	5	4	4	5												

KOALIB

This inventory

KOALIB [Tucker and Bryan 1966] [Niger-Iordofanian: Kordofanian: Koalib] [C Sudan (Nuba Hills); 24,000]

was included because of its five point occlusive contrast, its utilization of egressive and ingressive air streams and its rather elaborate vowel system.

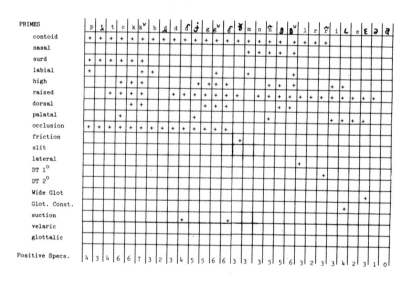

KOALIB -2

PRIMES	θ	ɔ	o	⍵	u	ɟ	ˀɟ	w																											
contoid																																				
nasal																																				
surd																																				
labial	+							+																												
high				+	+	+	+																													
raised	+	+	+	+	+	+	+	+																												
dorsal		+	+	+	+			+																												
palatal					+	+																														
occlusion																																				
friction																																				
slit																																				
lateral																																				
DT 1°																																				
DT 2°																																				
Wide Glot		+		+		+	+	+																												
Glot. Const.																																				
suction																																				
velaric																																				
glottalic						+																														
Positive Specs.	2	3	2	3	3	4	5	5																												

KUNG

This inventory

KUNG [Snyman 1970] [Koisan: Northern] [NE South West Africa: 10,000]

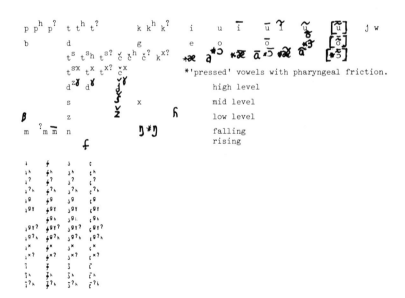

*'pressed' vowels with pharyngeal friction.

high level
mid level
low level
falling
rising

was included because it was the most elaborate of all inventories found in Ruhlen.

KUNG

PRIMES	p	pʰ	pˀ	t	tʰ	tˀ	k	kʰ	kˀ	b	d	g	tˢ	tˢʰ	tˢˀ	č	čʰ	čˀ	kˣ	tˢˣ	tˣ	tˣˀ	čˣ	dž	dˣ	ǰ	s	š	x	β
contoid	+	+	+	+	+	+	+	+	+	+	+	+	+	+	+	+	+	+	+	+	+	+	+	+	+	+	+	+	+	+
nasal																														
surd	+	+	+	+	+	+	+	+	+				+	+	+	+	+	+	+	+	+	+	+				+	+	+	
labial	+	+	+										+																	+
high					+	+	+			+				+	+	+	+					+			+		+	+		
raised				+	+	+	+	+	+		+	+	+	+	+	+	+	+	+	+	+	+	+	+	+		+	+		
dorsal					+	+	+			+									+	+	+	+	+	+	+			+		
palatal													+	+	+						+				+			+		
occlusion	+	+	+	+	+	+	+	+	+	+	+	+	+	+	+	+	+	+	+	+	+	+	+	+						
friction													+	+	+	+	+	+	+	+	+	+	+	+	+	+	+	+	+	+
slit																			+	+	+	+	+	+	+				+	
lateral																														
DT 1°													+	+	+	+	+	+	+	+	+	+	+	+	+	+				
DT 2°																			+			+	+	+		+				
Wide Glot		+			+			+						+			+													
Glot. Const.			+			+			+						+				+	+				+						
suction																														
velaric																														
glottalic																														
Positive Specs.	4	5	5	4	5	5	6	7	7	3	3	5	6	7	7	8	9	9	10	9	8	9	11	8	7	10	4	6	7	3

KUNG - 2

PRIMES	z	ž	ɦ	m	ʔm	m̄	n	ŋ	ʘ	ǂ	ǀ	ǀˀ	ǀ̃	ǀʰ	ǀ̰	ǁ	ǁˀ	ǁ̃	ǁʰ	ǁˣ	ǃ	ǃˀ	ǃ̃	ǃʰ	ǂʰ	ʘˀ	ʘʰ	ʘ̃	ʘˣ	ǂˀ
contoid	+	+		+	+	+	+	+	+	+	+	+	+	+	+	+	+	+	+	+	+	+	+	+	+	+	+	+	+	+
nasal				+	+	+	+	+															+	+	+					
surd											+	+	+	+					+	+	+	+	+	+	+	+				
labial				+	+	+		+																						
high		+						+	+																					
raised	+	+					+	+	+												+	+	+	+	+	+	+	+	+	+
dorsal							+	+							+	+		+	+										+	
palatal		+																												
occlusion									+	+	+	+	+	+	+	+	+	+	+	+	+	+	+	+	+	+	+	+	+	+
friction	+	+	+										+	+	+	+													+	
slit													+	+	+	+													+	
lateral																														
DT 1°				+	+								+	+	+	+													+	
DT 2°																														
Wide Glot									+		+				+				+		+	+				+				+
Glot. Const.				+						+					+	+	+				+			+	+	+				
suction									+	+	+	+	+	+	+	+	+	+	+	+	+	+	+	+	+	+	+	+	+	+
velaric									+	+	+	+	+	+	+	+	+	+	+	+	+	+	+	+	+	+	+	+	+	+
glottalic																														
Positive Specs.	3	5	1	3	5	4	3	5	6	1	5	6	6	6	4	8	9	6	9	10	6	7	8	6	6	7	8	5	9	6

KUNG - 3

PRIMES																														
contoid	+	+	+	+	+	+	+	+	+	+	+	+	+	+	+	+	+	+	+	+	+	+	+	+	+	+	+	+	+	+
nasal						+	+	+											+	+	+									
surd			+	+	+	+	+	+	+	+												+	+	+	+					
labial																														
high																				+	+	+	+	+	+	+	+	+	+	+
raised	+	+	+	+	+	+	+	+	+	+	+	+	+	+	+	+	+	+	+	+	+	+	+	+	+	+	+	+	+	+
dorsal	+		+	+									+	+	+	+	+	+									+		+	+
palatal																														
occlusion	+	+	+	+	+	+	+	+	+	+	+	+	+	+	+	+	+	+	+	+	+	+	+	+	+	+	+	+	+	+
friction	+		+	+									+		+		+	+									+		+	+
slit	+		+	+									+		+		+	+									+		+	+
lateral						+	+	+	+	+	+	+	+	+	+	+	+	+	+	+										
DT 1°	+		+	+									+	+	+	+	+	+									+		+	+
DT 2°																														
Wide Glot		+			+	+		+		+			+		+				+		+		+				+		+	+
Glot. Const.	+	+		+		+			+	+			+	+		+		+		+			+	+					+	+
suction	+	+	+	+	+	+	+	+	+	+	+	+	+	+	+	+	+	+	+	+	+	+	+	+	+	+	+	+	+	+
velaric	+	+	+	+	+	+	+	+	+	+	+	+	+	+	+	+	+	+	+	+	+	+	+	+	+	+	+	+	+	+
glottalic																														
Positive Specs.	10	7	10	11	7	8	9	7	8	8	9	6	10	9	11	10	10	11	7	8	8	7	8	8	9	6	10	7	11	12

KUNG - 4

PRIMES							i	e		a		o	u	ī		ā		ō	ū							J	v				
contoid	+	+	+	+	+																										
nasal			+	+	+												+	+	+	+	+	+	+								
surd	+	+	+	+	+																										
labial								+		+	+	+		+		+	+	+		+		+	+	+		+					
high	+	+	+	+	+	+				+	+			+	+				+	+				+	+	+					
raised	+	+	+	+	+	+	+			+	+	+	+		+	+	+	+				+	+	+	+	+					
dorsal	+	+								+	+	+			+	+	+					+	+	+		+					
palatal				+	+	+						+	+				+	+						+							
occlusion	+	+	+	+	+																										
friction	+	+						+		+				+		+			+		+										
slit	+	+																													
lateral																															
DT 1°	+	+								+	+	+	+	+	+	+															
DT 2°																															
Wide Glot			+	+						+					+			+		+			+	+							
Glot. Const.		+																													
suction	+	+	+	+	+																										
velaric	+	+	+	+	+																										
glottalic					+																										
Positive Specs.	11	12	8	9	10	3	2	3	0	5	3	4	4	1	6	4	5	4	5	1	6	4	5	4	5						

LAPP

The analysis of the Lapp phonological system (Kert, 1966) appears to present several difficulties for the distinctive feature set postulated here. Kert has established the following inventory:

LAPP [Kert 1966] [Uralic: Finno-Ugric: Lappic] [NW USSR (Kola Peninsula); 30,000]

$$
\begin{array}{llll}
p\ p^j\ \bar{p}\ \bar{p}^j & t\ \dot{t}\ t^j\ \bar{t}\ \bar{t}^j & k\ k^j\ \bar{k}\ \bar{k}^j & i\ \dot{\dotplus}\ u\ \bar{i} \\
b\ b^j\ \bar{b}\ \bar{b}^j & d\ \dot{d}\ d^j\ \bar{d}\ \bar{d}^j & g\ g^j\ \bar{g}\ \bar{g} & \varepsilon \\
\end{array}
$$

p p^j p̄ p̄^j   t ṫ t^j t̄ t̄^j   k k^j k̄ k̄^j   i ᵻ u ī   ū   j w (C)V(C)(C)
b b^j b̄ b̄^j   d ḋ d^j d̄ d̄^j   g g^j ḡ g̅   ɛ   o ɛ̄   ō   initial stress
          t^s t^sj t̄^s   ʒ^j ʒ̄^j   ə ɑ   ā ᾱ
          d^z d^zj   ɣ^j
f f^j f̄ f̄^j   s s^j s̄ s̄^j   š ʃ^j ʒ̄ ʒ̄ʲ x x^j x̄ x̄^j   h h^j h̄ h̄^j
v v^j v̄ v̄^j   z z^j z̄ z̄^j   ž ʒ^j ẓ ẓʲ
m m^j m̄ m̄^j   n ṅ n^j n̄ n̄^j   ŋ ŋ^j ŋ̄ ŋ̄ʲ   ṫ, ḋ, and ṅ are 'half-palatalized.'
          l l^j l̄ l̄^j
          r r^j r̄ r̄^j

Remarkable in this inventory is the number of segments that contrast in length and palatalization. The feature [length] of SPE has been discarded in favor of the utilization of the [delayed transition] features which are still sufficient to distinguish palatalized palatal affricates which are long or not long: /ǯ~ǯ̄/. This inventory contains /ṫ, ḋ, ṅ/ which are considered 'half palatalized'. I have chosen to contrast them as follows:

	t	ṫ	t^j	č
raised	+	+	+	+
high	–	+	–	+
palatal	–	–	+	+

The 'half-palatalized: sounds are specified the same way retroflex contoids in Indian languages are, [+high] but [–palatal] and [–dorsal]. This system claims that no language contrasts retroflex and 'half-palatalized' contoids.

In order to distinguish palatalized contoids from non-palatalized ones, I have employed the feature [palatal] without its (usually)

concommitant feature [high] which is used to indicate palatal contoids. This, then, establishes a distinction between contoids with
palatal timber, m^j, t^j, k^j, etc. and contoids articulated in the palatal
area such as š, ž, č, etc. Palatized contoids are not complex in the same
way affricates are, i.e., they are not positively specified for [delayed
transition], because, contrary to affricates, they cannot be considered
two contoids which pattern as a unit. The following matrix illustrates
distinctions among, palatal, palatalized, and non-palatal segments:

	m	m^j	t	t^j	x	x^j	s	$š^j$	$\bar{š}^{j1}$
nasal	+	+	–	–	–	–	–	–	–
occl	–	–	+	+	–.	–	–	–	–
fric	–	–	–	–	+	+	+	+	+
labial	+	+	–	–	–	–	–	–	–
high	–	–	–	–	+	+	+	+	+
dorsal	–	–	–	–	+	+	–	–	–
palatal	–	+	–	+	–	+	–	+	+
D.T.	–	–	–	–	–	–	–	–	+

Palatalization, I have claimed, is a *timbre* rather than a palatal
contoidal articulation. The specification [+palatal] for non-palatal,
palatalized segments suffices to distinguish them from ordinary non-
palatal contoids just as a specification such as [+palatal, +high,
+contoid, +labial] would identify segments such as $ñ^w$ which would
contrast with m^j. This system can contrast x^j with $š^x$ (a velarized
palatal) by specifying the first as [+dorsal, +slit, +palatal], the second
as [+palatal, +dorsal, –slit], thus they can be contrasted in this system if
someday someone finds such segments in a language.

The contrast $/č^j \sim \check{č}^j/$ is not really problematic: $/č^j/$ is specified twice
for palatal and once for [delayed transition]; $/\check{č}^j/$ is specified for both
[D.T. 1, 2] and twice for [palatal]. In the Lapp inventory the
palatalized quality of these palatal affricates is redundant, since they
do not contrast with non-palatalized affricates—but, if they did, they
could be distinguished from such segments using the strategem of
double marking for [palatal].

LAPP

PRIMES	p	pʲ	p̄	p̄ʲ	t	t̰	tʲ	t̄	t̄ʲ	k	kʲ	k̄	k̄ʲ	b	bʲ	b̄	b̄ʲ	d	d̰	dʲ	d̄	d̄ʲ	g	gʲ	ḡ	ḡʲ	ts	tsʲ	t̄s	c̄ʲ
contoid	+	+	+	+	+	+	+	+	+	+	+	+	+	+	+	+	+	+	+	+	+	+	+	+	+	+	+	+	+	+
nasal																														
surd	+	+	+	+	+	+	+	+	+	+	+	+	+														+	+	+	+
labial	+	+	+	+										+	+	+	+													
high						+				+	+	+	+						+				+	+	+	+				+
raised					+	+	+	+	+	+	+	+				+	+	+	+	+	+	+	+	+	+	+	+	+	+	+
dorsal										+	+	+	+										+	+	+	+				
palatal		+		+		+		+		+		+		+		+			+		+		+		+			+		++
occlusion	+	+	+	+	+	+	+	+	+	+	+	+	+	+	+	+	+	+	+	+	+	+	+	+	+	+	+	+	+	+
friction																											+	+	+	+
slit																														
lateral																														
DT 1°		+	+			+	+			+	+			+	+			+	+			+	+	+	+	+	+
DT 2°																													+
Wide Glot																														
Glot. Const.																														
suction																														
velaric																														
glottalic																														
Positive Specs.	4	5	5	6	4	5	5	5	6	6	6	7	7	8	3	4	4	5	3	4	4	4	5	5	6	6	7	6	7	7	9

LAPP -2

PRIMES	c̄ʲ	dᶻ	dᶻʲ	ɟʲ	f	fʲ	f̄	f̄ʲ	s	sʲ	s̄	s̄ʲ	š	šʲ	ž̄	ž̄ʲ	x	xʲ	x̄	x̄ʲ	v	vʲ	v̄	v̄ʲ	z	zʲ	z̄	z̄ʲ	ž	žʲ
contoid	+	+	+	+	+	+	+	+	+	+	+	+	+	+	+	+	+	+	+	+	+	+	+	+	+	+	+	+	+	±
nasal																														
surd	+				+	+	+	+	+	+	+	+	+	+	+	+	+	+	+	+										
labial																					+	+	+	+						
high	+			+							+	+	+	+	+	+	+	+											+	+
raised	+	+	+	+					+	+	+	+	+	+	+	+	+	+							+	+	+	+	+	++
dorsal																	+	+	+	+										
palatal	++		+	++		+		+		+		+	+	++	+	++		+		+		+		+		+		+	+	+
occlusion	+	+	+	+																										
friction	+	+	+	+	+	+	+	+	+	+	+	+	+	+	+	+	+	+	+	+	+	+	+	+	+	+	+	+	+	+
slit					+	+	+	+													+	+	+	+						
lateral																														
DT 1°	+	+	+	+			+	+			+	+			+	+			+	+			+	+			+	+	
DT 2°	+																													
Wide Glot																														
Glot. Const.																														
suction																														
velaric																														
glottalic																														
Positive Specs.	10	5	6	8	4	5	5	6	4	5	5	6	6	7	7	8	6	7	7	8	4	5	5	6	3	4	4	5	5	6

Appendix A 99

LAPP -3

PRIMES	ɣ̄	ɣ̄ʲ	m	mʲ	m̄	m̄ʲ	n	nʲ	n̄	n̄ʲ	ŋ	ŋʲ	ŋ̄	ŋ̄ʲ	l	lʲ	l̄	l̄ʲ	r	rʲ	r̄	r̄ʲ	h	hʲ	h̄	h̄ʲ	i	ɛ	a
contoid	+	+	+	+	+	+	+	+	+	+	+	+	+	+	+	+	+	+	+	+	+								
nasal			+	+	+	+	+	+	+	+	+	+	+	+															
surd																							+	+	+	+			
labial			+	+	+	+																							
high	+	+							+				+	+	+	+												+	
raised	+	+			+	+	+	+	+	+	+	+	+	+	+	+	+	+	+	+	+						+	+	
dorsal											+	+	+	+															
palatal	+	+		+		+			+			+	+		+		+		+		+		+		+		+	+	+
occlusion																													
friction	+	+																					+	+	+	+			
slit																													
lateral															+	+	+	+											
DT 1°	+	+			+	+			+	+		+			+		+			+		+			+	+			
DT 2°																													
Wide Glot																													
Glot. Const.																													
suction																													
velaric																													
glottalic																													
Positive Specs.	6	6	3	4	4	5	3	4	4	4	5	5	6	6	7	3	4	4	5	2	3	3	4	2	3	3	4	3	2	0

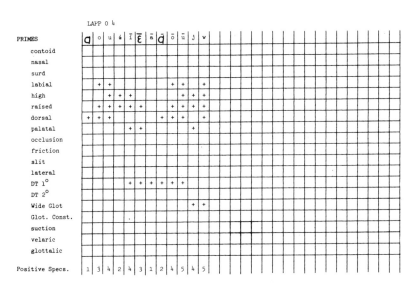

LAPP 0 4

PRIMES	ɑ	o	u	ɨ	ɪ	ɛ̄	ā	ɖ	ō	ū	ɟ	w
contoid												
nasal												
surd												
labial		+	+				+	+			+	
high			+	+	+				+	+	+	
raised		+	+	+	+	+			+	+	+	+
dorsal	+	+	+				+	+	+		+	
palatal				+	+						+	
occlusion												
friction												
slit												
lateral												
DT 1°				+	+	+	+	+	+			
DT 2°												
Wide Glot								+	+			
Glot. Const.												
suction												
velaric												
glottalic												
Positive Specs.	1	3	4	2	4	3	1	2	4	5	4	5

MURA

This inventory

MURA (Piraha) [Sheldon 1974] [Macro-Chibchan:–] [W Brazil (Amazonas); 100]

p	t	k	?	i		high	SOV/NA
b		g			o	mid	
	s		h	a		low	

was included because it was the smallest of all inventories and contains no nasals, laterals or vibrants.

MURA

PRIMES	p	t	k	?	b	g	s	h	i	a	o
contoid	+	+	+		+	+	+				
nasal											
surd	+	+	+	+			+	+			
labial											
high											
raised		+	+				+		+		
dorsal			+			+		+			
palatal											
occlusion											
friction						+	+				
slit											
lateral											
DT 1°											
DT 2°											
Wide Glot											
Glot. Const.											
suction											
velaric											
glottalic											
Positive Specs.	2	3	4	1	1	3	4	2	1	0	2

NORWEGIAN

This inventory

NORWEGIAN (Standard Eastern) [Vanvik 1972] [Indo-European:
Germanic: North] [Norway; 4.3 million]

p	ƚ̣	ț	k	[?]		i	y	ʉ̄	u	ī	ȳ	ʉ̄ ū		j	w	high
b	d̂	ḍ̇	g			e	ø	ə	ɔ	ē	ø̄	ɔ̄				low
f		s	ṣ̌	ç	h		æ	ɑ		ǣ	ɑ̄					
m	n̂	ṇ̇		ʝ												SVO/AN
	l̂	ḷ̇														
	ɽ															

is a rather elaborate Indo-European language with the interesting
contrast of /ç/ and /š/ where [slit] and [groove] or [±dorsal] fricatives
contrast in the palatal region.

NORWEGIAN

PRIMES	p	ƚ̣	ț	k	b	d̂	ḍ̇	g	f	s	ṣ̌	ç	h	m	n̂	ṇ̇	ʝ	λ	l	ɽ	i	ü	e	ö	æ	a	ʉ	ə	ɔ	ʉ
contoid	+	+	+	+	+	+	+	+	+	+	+	+		+	+	+	+	+	+	+										
nasal														+	+	+	+													
surd	+	+	+	+					+	+	+	+	+																	
labial	+				+								+									+		+		+		+	+	+
high		+	+			+	+			+	+			+	+		+		+	+	+			+			+			
raised		+	+			+	+		+	+	+			+	+		+		+		+	+	+	+			+	+	+	+
dorsal			+				+									+											+	+		
palatal									+		+						+	+	+	+	+									
occlusion	+	+	+	+	+	+	+	+																						
friction									+	+	+	+	+																	
slit									+			+																		
lateral																		+	+											
DT 1°																														
DT 2°																														
Wide Glot																														
Glot. Const.																														
suction																														
velaric																														
glottalic																														
Positive Specs.	4	3	5	6	3	2	4	5	4	4	6	7	2	3	2	4	5	2	4	1	3	4	2	3	1	0	3	1	3	4

NORWEGIAN - 2

PRIMES	ĭ	ū	ē	ŏ	ʀ̄	a	ɔ̄	ū	ü	J	w																					
contoid																																
nasal																																
surd																																
labial		+		+			+	+	+		+																					
high	+	+						+	+	+	+																					
raised	+	+	+	+			+	+	+	+	+																					
dorsal							+	+			+																					
palatal	+	+	+	+	+					+																						
occlusion																																
friction																																
slit																																
lateral																																
DT 1°	+	+	+	+	+	+	+	+	+																							
DT 2°																																
Wide Glot										+	+																					
Glot. Const.																																
suction																																
velaric																																
glottalic																																
Positive Specs.	4	5	3	4	2	1	4	5	4	4	5																					

NUNGGUBUYU

This rather sparse inventory

NUNGGUBUYU [Hughes and Leeding 1971] [Australian: Nunggubuyuan]
[NC Australia (NE Northern Territory); 400]

```
p  t̪  t  ṭ  c  k      ɭ      wᵛ            j  w     (C)V(C)(C)

m  [n]  n  ṇ  ɲ  ŋ              e                     stress on long
   l̪   l  ḷ                              ā            vowels; otherwise
                                                      initial
        r  ɽ
                                                      SOV/NA
```

was included for its simplicity, but also because of the six point
contrasts in stops. SPE DF's cannot distinguish / p t̪ t ṭ c k /:

	p	t̪	t	ṭ	c	k
sonorant						
vocalic						
consonantal	+	+	+	+	+	+
coronal		+	+	+	+	
anterior	+	+	+	+		
distributed			+		+	+
covered						
nasal						
glot. const.						
lateral						
high				+	+	+
low						

unless one uses the feature [distributed] for /c/ and /t/ and /high/ for /t/ contrary to Harris (1969).

NUNGGUBUYU

PRIMES	p	t̪	t	ṭ	c	k	m	n	ṇ	ñ	ŋ	ḻ	l	ḷ	r	ɥ	ʟ	ʔ	v̌	ā	J	v
contoid	+	+	+	+	+	+	+	+	+	+	+	+	+	+	+							
nasal							+	+	+	+	+											
surd																						
labial	+						+															+
high			+	+	+				+	+	+			+		+	+	+		+	+	
raised			+	+	+	+		+	+	+	+		+	+	+	+	+	+		+	+	
dorsal						+					+						+				+	
palatal					+					+						+			+			
occlusion	+	+	+	+	+	+																
friction																						
slit																						
lateral												+	+	+								
DT 1°																			+			
DT 2°																						
Wide Glot																				+	+	
Glot. Const.																						
suction																						
velaric																						
glottalic																						
Positive Specs.	3	2	3	4	5	5	3	3	4	5	5	2	3	4	2	3	3	0	3	1	4	5

URDU

This inventory

URDU [Bender 1967] [Indo-European: Indic] [Pakistan; 40 million]

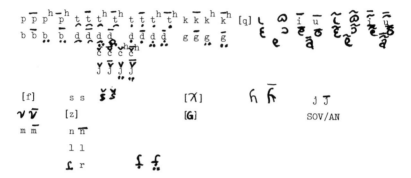

[f]　　　s s　　　š ž　　　　　　　[χ]　　　　ɦ ɦ̄　　　ɟ ɟ̄

v v̄　　[z]　　　　　　　　　　　[ɢ]

m m̄　　　　n n̄

　　　　　　l l

　　　　　ɽ r　　　　ɸ ɸ̈

was included partially because of its elaboration and partially because of the occlusive contrasts such as /p~pʰ~b~bʰ/ which are specified using my system through the presence or absence of a wide glottal opening. Using the Chomsky-Halle D.F.'s, the voiced aspirates are handled by an additional feature, [heightened subglottalic pressure].

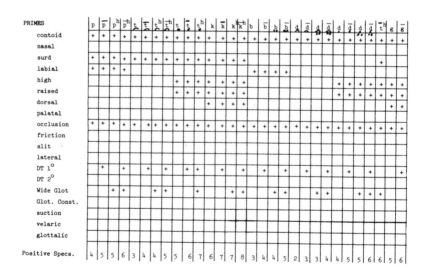

URDU -2

PRIMES	g	ḡ	č	č̌	čh	č̌h	y	ȳ	y̰	ȳ̰	s	s̄	ž	ž̄	v	ṽ	m	m̄	n	n̄	l	l̄	ɾ	r	ʄ	ʄ̣	ɦ	ɦ̄	ʊ	ʕ
contoid	+	+	+	+	+	+	+	+	+	+	+	+	+	+	+	+	+	+	+	+	+	+	+	+	+	+				
nasal																	+	+	+	+										
surd			+	+	+	+					+	+	+	+																
labial															+	+	+	+												
high	+	+	+	+	+	+	+	+	+	+			+	+											+	+			+	
raised	+	+	+	+	+	+	+	+	+	+	+	+	+	+					+	+					+	+	+			+	+
dorsal	+	+																												
palatal			+	+	+	+	+	+	+	+			+	+															+	+
occlusion	+	+	+	+	+	+	+	+	+	+																				
friction			+	+	+	+	+	+	+	+	+	+	+	+													+	+		
slit																														
lateral																					+	+								
DT 1°			+	+	+	+	+	+	+	+			+		+	+,		+		+			+						+	
DT 2°				+		+		+		+																				
Wide Glot	+	+			+	+			+	+																	+			
Glot. Const.																														
suction																														
velaric																														
glottalic																														
Positive Specs.	6	7	8	9	9	10	7	8	8	9	4	5	6	7	2	3	3	4	3	4	2	3	1	2	3	4	1	2	3	2

URDU -3

PRIMES	e	ɔ	ɶ	ī	ē	ā	ō	ū	ĩ	ẽ	ã	ɔ̃	õ	ĩ̄	ẽ̄	æ̃	ȭ	ũ̄	J	J̄
contoid																				
nasal									+	+	+	+	+	+	+	+	+	+		
surd																				
labial		+	+		+	+			+	+			+	+						
high		+	+		+	+			+	+			+	+	+					
raised	+	+	+	+	+	+	+	+	+	+	+	+	+	+	+					
dorsal	+	+			+	+			+	+			+	+						
palatal		+	+		+	+			+	+			+	+						
occlusion																				
friction																				
slit																				
lateral																				
DT 1°		+	+	+	+	+			+	+	+	+	+		+					
DT 2°																				
Wide Glot													+	+						
Glot. Const.																				
suction																				
velaric																				
glottalic																				
Positive Specs.	0	3	4	4	3	1	4	5	4	3	1	4	5	5	4	2	5	6	4	5

Footnotes

[1]Professor Ernie Scatton of the Slavic Language Department of SUNY Albany has informed me (personal communication) of a tendency among Soviet researchers to over-elaborate the segmental inventories of the languages they investigate. Indeed, the long segments of this inventory could be analyzed as sequences, the palatalized as *C+j*. This would reduce the inventory to 33 segments. Hasselbrink (1965:6,20) postulates 28 phonemes for this language. He examines the virtues of analyzing palatalized consonants as units, sequences of contoid plus vocoid or as contoids modified by suprasegmentals. He decides upon a suprasegmental analysis, but such an analysis is not consonant with the phonetic theory involved here—it has no articulatory motivation. The solution that I use, considering palatalization a *timbre* rather than a contoidal articulation is implicitly suprasegmental inasmuch as [palatal] articulation may be added to any other sound. Obviously, the exact configuration of the tongue will vary according to the segment that is being palatalized.

Epilogue to Appendix A:
The Non-Universality of the
Phonetic Parameters

Earlier (Chapter II) I suggested that to constitute marks each of these parameters should be unnecessary in some phonological system; if they were universal, they would not be marks, they would be backdrops. Let us examine the features used in specifying the segments in the systems examined in this appendix in order to see if each feature is dispensable in one or another inventory's specification.

Non Controversial, Non Universal Features. Seven of the features of this inventory are uncontroversially non-universal. They are: [D.T. 1 and 2, Widened Glottis, Glottal Constriction, Suction, Velaric, Glottalic]. There are many languages that have neither affricates nor long segments therefore [D.T. 1 and 2] are not universal. Many languages have neither lax vowels nor tense contoids, thus [widened glottis] is not universal. Laryngeal creak, indicated by [glottal constriction] is rare, as are implosives, clicks, and glottalic segments.

Jakobson (see chapter II) held consonant vowel, here [contoid] and vocoid, to be universal categories. The segments of Aleut can be contrastively specified without using the feature [contoid].

Nasal. [Nasal] is not a necessary specification in the phonological system of Mura.

Surd. [Surd] is not a necessary parameter of the Dyirbal, Gadsup or Nunggabuyu phonemic inventories.

Labial. [Labial] is not necessry to specify and contrast the sounds in Mura or in Cherokee.

High. [High] is not a necessary feature in the systems of Mura, Gadsup, and Alabaman.

Raised is not necessary in Andoa and Aleut.

Dorsal is not necessry in Andoa.

Palatal is not necessary in Gadsup.

Occlusion is not necessary in Cherokee.

Friction is not necessary in Alabaman or Gadsup.

Slit is not necessary in Gadsup.

Lateral is not necessary in Mura.

The evidence presented here suggests that the features proposed in this treatise are truly marks, since they work in specifying phonemic inventories of extreme complexity and divergent configuration, but, at the same time, no one parameter is necessary in all phonological systems.

Appendix B
Revised, *SPE,* and *PSA* Specifications of the Representative Segmental Inventory

As one can see by comparing the representative inventory to the inventories of some of the languages in Appendix A, there is more complexity than was originally postulated in the section on segmental strength. The most complex segments used in this inventory were k^{xh} and $k^{x'}$, aspirated and glottalized dorsal affricates with ten positive specifications each. There were several languages with segments needing ten positive specifications: /č̆ʰ/ of Urdu, /ɔ̆ʲ/ of Lapp, and some of the clicks in ǀko and Kung. The following segments of Kung needed eleven: /ʄˣˀ/ /ʄᶢˠˀ/, /ʃˣˀ/ and /č̆ˣˀ/. The existence of very few segments needing more than ten positive specifications suggests that the averages extracted from the specifications of the anthropophonic representations are reasonably representative of what linguists are likely to find in future investigations.

PRIMES	p	t	ṭ	c	k	x	ʔ	pʰ	tʰ	ṭʰ	cʰ	kʰ	p'	t'	ṭ'	c'	k'	q	ʈ	ɽ	ɭ	pp	ts	tʂ	ɣ	kˣ	ppʰ	tsʰ	tʂʰ	ɣʰ
contoid	+	+	+	+	+	+		+	+	+	+	+	+	+	+	+	+	+	+	+	+	+	+	+	+	+	+	+	+	+
nasal																														
surd	+	+	+	+	+	+	+	+	+	+	+	+	+	+	+	+	+	+	+	+	+	+	+	+	+	+	+	+	+	+
labial	+							+					+						+			+				+				
high			+	+	+				+	+	+			+	+	+			+	+			+	+			+	+
raised		+	+	+	+	+			+	+	+	+		+	+	+	+		+	+	+		+	+	+	+		+	+	+
dorsal				+	+						+					+									+				
palatal				+							+					+					+				+					+
occlusion	+	+	+	+	+	+	+	+	+	+	+	+	+	+	+	+	+	+	+	+	+	+	+	+	+	+	+	+	+	+
friction																						+	+	+	+	+	+	+	+	+
slit																									+					
lateral																														
DT 1°																						+	+	+	+	+	+	+	+	+
DT 2°																														
Wide Glot								+	+	+	+	+															+	+	+	+
Glot. Const.																														
suction																			+	+	+	+									
velaric																			+	+	+	+									
glottalic													+	+	+	+	+													
Positive Specs.	4	4	5	6	6	5	2	5	5	6	7	7	5	5	6	7	7	6	6	7	8	6	6	7	8	9	7	7	8	9

PRIMES	kˣ	ppʼ	tsʼ	tʂʼ	c'	kˣʼ	tl	ṭl	ct	pʷ	tʷ	ṭʷ	cʷ	kʷ	ʼp	ʼt	ʼc	ʼk	ɗ	ɗ	ɗ	b	d	ḍ	ɟ	g	Gʰ	bʰ	dʰ	dʰ
contoid	+	+	+	+	+	+	+	+	+	+	+	+	+	+	+	+	+	+	+	+	+	+	+	+	+	+	+	+	+	+
nasal																														
surd	+	+	+	+	+	+	+	+	+	+	+	+	+	+	+	+	+	+	+											
labial		+								++	+	+	+	+						+					+					
high	+			+	+	+		+	+		+	+	+		+	+		+	+				+	+	+					+
raised	+		+	+	+	+	+	+		+	+	+		+	+	+	+	+		+	+	+	+	+		+	+
dorsal	+				+			+				+			+			+							+	+				
palatal			+				+			+			+			+				+				+						
occlusion	+	+	+	+	+	+	+	+	+	+	+	+	+	+	+	+	+	+	+	+	+	+	+	+	+	+	+	+	+	+
friction	+	+	+	+	+	+																								
slit	+				+																									
lateral							+	+	+																					
DT 1°	+	+	+	+	+	+																								
DT 2°																														
Wide Glot	+										+	+	+	+													+	+	+
Glot. Const.											+	+	+	+															
suction															+	+	+												
velaric															+	+	+												
glottalic		+	+	+	+	+																								
Positive Specs.	10	7	7	8	9	10	5	6	7	5	5	6	7	7	6	6	8	8	7	8	9	3	3	4	5	5	4	4	4	5

PRIMES (top table)

PRIMES	jʰ	gʰ	bʙ	dz	dʑ	ɣ	gʲ	dl	dⱡ	ɟ1	bʷ	dʷ	dʲ	jʷ	gʷ	ʕ	ɗ	ʄ	ʃ	gʼ	bm	dn	dŋ	ɟɲ	gn	bmb	dnd	dnɖ	ɟnɟ	gng
contoid	+	+	+	+	+	+	+	+	+	+	+	+	+	+	+	+	+	+	+	+	+	+	+	+	+	+	+	+	+	+
nasal																					+	+	+	+	+	+	+	+	+	+
surd																														
labial			+								++	+	+	+	+	+					+					+				
high	+	+			+	+	+		+	+			+	+	+			+	+	+			+	+	+			+	+	+
raised	+	+		+	+	+	+	+	+	+		+	+	+	+		+	+	+	+		+	+	+	+		+	+	+	+
dorsal		+					+			+					+				+				+							+
palatal	+				+				+				+						+				+							+
occlusion	+	+	+	+	+	+	+	+	+	+	+	+	+	+	+	+	+	+	+	+	+	+	+	+	+	+	+	+	+	+
friction			+	+	+	+	+			+																				
slit							+																							
lateral								+	+	+																				
DT 1°			+	+	+	+	+																			+	+	+	+	+
DT 2°																		✝	+	+	+	+								
Wide Glot	+	+																												
Glot. Const.																	.													
suction																	+	+	+	+	+									
velaric																														
glottalic																														
Positive Specs.	6	6	5	5	6	7	8	4	5	6	4	4	5	6	6	4	4	5	6	6	5	5	6	7	7	5	5	6	7	7

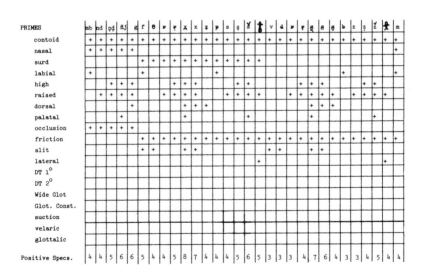

PRIMES (bottom table)

PRIMES	mb	nd	ɳɖ	ɲɟ	gʼ	f	θ	ʋ	ɸ	x	ʒ	ʂ	s	ʂ	ɣ	ʈ	v	ð	ɹ	ɣ	ʁ	ʐ	ʑ	b	z	ʐ	ʑ	ʈ	m
contoid	+	+	+	+	+	+	+	+	+	+	+	+	+	+	+	+	+	+	+	+	+	+	+	+	+	+	+	+	+
nasal	+	+	+	+	+																								+
surd						+	+	+	+	+	+	+	+	+	+														
labial	+					+							+											+					+
high			+	+	+			+	+	+				+	+					+	+	+				+	+		
raised		+	+	+	+			+	+	+			+	+	+	+			+	+	+	+	+		+	+	+	+	
dorsal			+					+	+	+									+	+	+								
palatal				+					+					+					+				+						
occlusion	+	+	+	+	+																								
friction						+	+	+	+	+	+	+	+	+	+	+	+	+	+	+	+	+	+	+	+	+	+	+	+
slit						+	+			+	+						+	+			+	+							
lateral														+														+	
DT 1°																													
DT 2°																													
Wide Glot																													
Glot. Const.																													
suction																													
velaric																													
glottalic																													
Positive Specs.	4	4	5	6	6	5	4	4	5	8	7	4	4	4	5	6	5	3	3	3	4	7	6	4	3	3	4	5	4	4

PRIMES	n	ñ	ŋ	l	l̃	ʎ	r	r̃	R	ᶦ	e	ɛ	æ	I	ü	ö	ɔ̈	ə	ɨ	ɟ	ï	ë	ɛ̈	U	u	o	ɔ	a
contoid	+	+	+	+	+	+	+	+	+																			
nasal	+	+	+																									
surd																												
labial															+	+	+							+	+	+	+	
high		+	+		+	+		+							+	+	+				+	+						
raised	+	+	+	+	+	+	+	+	+	+	+	+		+	+	+	+	+	+	+	+	+	+	+	+	+	+	+
dorsal		+			+		+													+	+	+	+	+	+	+	+	+
palatal	+			+				+	+	+	+	+		+	+	+												
occlusion																												
friction																												
slit																												
lateral				+	+	+																						
DT 1°								+																				
DT 2°																												
Wide Glot											+		+				+		+				+	+			+	
Glot. Const.																												
suction																												
velaric																												
glottalic																												
Positive Specs.	3	5	5	3	5	5	2	3	3	3	2	3	1	3	4	3	4	1	3	2	3	2	3	5	4	3	4	0

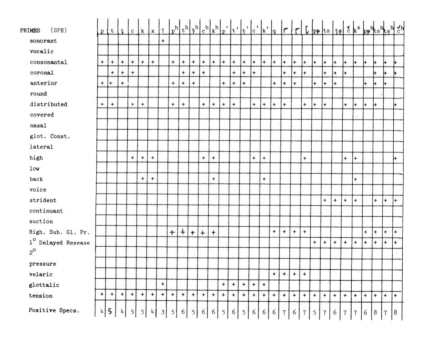

PRIMES (SPE)	p	t	ţ	c	k	x	ʔ	pʰ	tʰ	ţʰ	cʰ	kʰ	pʼ	tʼ	ţʼ	cʼ	kʼ	q	ɾ	ɽ	ʕ	pᵖ	ts	ţs	c̣	kˣ	pᵇ	ţsʰ	kˣʰ	cʰ
sonorant							+																							
vocalic																														
consonantal	+	+	+	+	+	+		+	+	+	+	+	+	+	+	+	+	+	+	+	+	+	+	+	+	+	+	+	+	+
coronal		+	+	+					+	+	+			+	+	+			+	+	+		+	+				+	+	+
anterior	+	+	+					+	+	+			+	+	+				+	+	+		+	+				+	+	+
round																														
distributed	+	+		+	+			+	+		+	+	+	+		+	+		+	+	+		+	+	+	+		+	+	+
covered																														
nasal																														
glot. Const.																														
lateral																														
high			+	+	+					+	+				+	+			+				+	+						+
low																														
back				+	+						+					+			+					+						
voice																														
strident																						+	+	+	+		+	+	+	+
continuant																														
suction																														
High. Sub. Gl. Pr.								+	+	+	+	+							+	+	+	+						+	+	+
1° Delayed Resease																							+	+	+	+	+	+	+	+
2°																														
pressure																														
velaric																		+	+	+	+									
glottalic							+						+	+	+	+	+													
tension	+	+	+	+	+	+	+	+	+	+	+	+	+	+	+	+	+	+	+	+	+	+	+	+	+	+	+	+	+	+
Positive Specs.	4	5	4	5	5	4	3	5	6	5	6	6	5	6	5	6	6	6	7	6	7	5	7	6	7	7	6	8	7	8

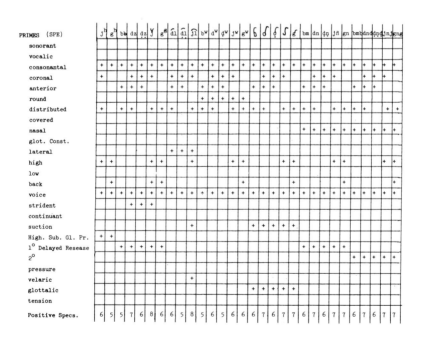

First chart

PRIMES (SPE)	mb	nd	ñɟ	ng	f	θ	ᵽ	p̪	x̄	x	x̌	ᵽ	s	ṣ	š	ǳ̌	v	đ	ᵽ	ř	g̊	ʁ	ᶢ	ꝗ	b	z	ẓ	ž	ǰ	m
sonorant																														+
vocalic																														
consonantal	+	+	+	+	+	+	+	+	+	+	+	+	+	+	+	+	+	+	+	+	+	+	+	+	+	+	+	+	+	+
coronal		+	+				+	+				+	+	+	+			+	+							+	+	+	+	
anterior	+	+			+	+	+	+				+	+	+		+	+	+	+	+						+	+	+		
round																														
distributed	+	+	+	+		⌐	+			+		+	+		+	+				+			+			+	+		+	+	+
covered																						+								
nasal	+	+	+	+																										+
glot. Const.																+													+	
lateral																														
high		+	+				+	+				+							+	+							+			
low			+																											
back			+				+	+	+										+	+	+									
voice	+	+	+	+													+	+	+	+	+	+	+	+	+	+	+	+	+	+
strident			+	+			+	+	+		+	+	+	+	+	+	+									+	+	+	+	
continuant			+	+	+	+	+	+	+	+	+	+	+	+	+	+	+	+	+	+	+	+	+	+	+	+	+	+	+	
suction																														
High. Sub. Gl. Pr.																														
1° Delayed Resease				+	+	+	+	+	+	+	+	+	+	+	+	+	+	+	+	+	+	+	+	+	+	+	+	+	+	
2°																														
pressure																														
velaric																														
glottalic																															
tension				+	+	+	+	+	+	+	+	+	+	+																
Positive Specs.	5	6	6	6	6	7	7	6	7	8	6	6	8	7	8	9	6	6	7	6	6	7	5	5	6	8	7	8	8	5

Second chart

PRIMES (SPE)	n	ñ	ŋ	l	ĺ	ĺ̃	r	r̃	R	i	e	ɛ	æ	I	ü	ö	ɔ̈	ə	ɨ	ɟ	I	ë	ë̃	U	u	o	ɔ	a	y	ɰ
sonorant	+	+	+	+	+	+	+	+	+	+	+	+	+	+	+	+	+	+	+	+	+	+	+	+	+	+	+	+	+	+
vocalic				+	+	+				+	+	+	+	+	+	+	+	+	+	+	+	+	+	+	+	+	+	+	−	−
consonantal	+	+	+	+	+	+	+	+	+																				−	−
coronal	+	+		+	+		+	+											+										+	
anterior	+	+		+	+		+	+		+	+	+	+	+	+	+													+	
round															+	+	+													+
distributed	+	+	+	+	+	+																								
covered																														
nasal	+	+	+																											
glot. Const.																														
lateral				+	+	+																								
high	+	+		+	+		+	+						+	+				+		+			+	+				+	+
low													+															+		
back							+									+	+	+	+					+	+	+	+		+	
voice	+	+	+	+	+	+	+	+	+	+	+	+	+	+	+	+	+	+	+	+	+	+	+	+	+	+	+	+	+	+
strident																														
continuant				+	+	+	+	+	+	+	+	+	+	+	+	+	+	+	+	+	+	+	+	+	+	+	+	+	+	+
suction																														
High. Sub. Gl. Pr.																														
1° Delayed Resease																														
2°																														
pressure																														
velaric																														
glottalic																															
tension							+	+	+	+		+		+	+	+			+	+			+	+						
Positive Specs.	7	8	6	9	10	8	6	7	7	7	6	5	7	6	8	7	7	4	5	5	7	6	5	6	7	6	5	6	5	6

PRIMES (PSA)	p	t	t̤	c	k	x	ʔ	pʰ	tʰ	t̤ʰ	cʰ	kʰ	p	t	t̤	c	k	q	f	f̤	C	pp	ts	t̤s	c	kˣ	pp	ts	t̤s	č	kˣ
consonantal	+	+	+	+	+	+		+	+	+	+	+	+	+	+	+	+	+	+	+	+	+	+	+	+	+	+	+	+	+	+
nasal																															
surd	+	+	+	+	+	+	+	+	+	+	+	+	+	+	+	+	+	+	+	+	+	+	+	+	+	+	+	+	+	+	+
compact			+	+	+					+	+				+	+								+	+					+	+
nondiffuse				+																											
grave	+			+	+		+			+	+				+	+			+					+	+						+
flat		+							+					+						+					+						+
sharp			+								+				+					+					+						+
interr.	+	+	+	+	+	+	+	+	+	+	+	+	+	+	+	+	+	+	+	+	+	+	+	+	+	+	+	+	+	+	+
friction																			+	+	+	+	+	+	+	+	+	+	+	+	+
slit																						+	+					+	+		
lateral																															
DT 1°																						+	+	+	+	+	+	+	+	+	+	+
DT 2°																						+	+								
wide glot.								+	+	+	+	+															+	+	+	+	+
checked									+					+	+	+	+	+													
suction																															
velaric																		+	+	+	+											
glottalic																															
Pos. Specs.	4	3	4	5	5	6	3	5	4	5	6	6	5	4	5	6	6	5	4	5	4	6	5	6	8	8	7	6	7	9	9

PRIMES (PSA)	pp	ts	t̤s	č	kˣ	tl	t̤l	cl	pʷ	tʷ	t̤ʷ	cʷ	kʷ	*p	*ɨ	*c	*k	č	c̣	č̣	b	d	d̤	ɟ	g	G	bʰ	dʰ	d̤ʰ	ɟʰ	gʰ
consonantal	+	+	+	+	+	+	+	+	+	+	+	+	+	+	+	+	+	+	+	+	+	+	+	+	+	+	+	+	+	+	+
nasal																															
surd	+	+	+	+	+	+	+	+	+	+	+	+	+	+	+	+	+	+	+	+											
compact			+	+				+			+	+			+	+				+	+	+							+	+
nondiffuse																															
grave	+			+				+			+	+			+				+				+	+	+					+
flat		+			+	+	+	+	+			+						+						+					
sharp			+			+			+			+						+						+				
interr.	+	+	+	+	+	+	+	+	+	+	+	+	+	+	+	+	+	+	+	+	+	+	+	+	+	+	+	+	+	+	+
friction	+	+	+	+	+																										
slit			+	+																											
lateral					+	+	+																								
DT 1°	+	+	+	+	+																										
DT 2°																															
wide glot.									+	+	+	+												+	+	+	+	+
checked	+	+	+	+					+	+	+	+																	
suction									+	+	+																		
velaric																															
glottalic									+	+	+																				
Pos. Specs.	6	6	7	9	9	4	5	6	5	4	4	6	6	6	5	7	7	5	5	5	3	2	3	4	4	4	4	3	4	5	5

PRIMES (PSA)

	bʰ	dz	dz̧	ɣ	gˠ	dl	dl̦	ɲ̃	bʷ	dʷ	dˠ	jˠ	gʷ	ʕ	ʄ	ɗ	ʛ	g	bm	dn	dn̦	ɲ̃	gŋ	bmbdndn̦ɲgŋ	mb	nd	nd
consonantal	+	+	+	+	+	+	+	+	+	+	+	+	+	+	+	+	+	+	+	+	+	+	+	+	+	+	+
nasal																			+	+	+	+	+	+	+	+	+
surd																											
compact			+	+							+	+				+	+				+	+			+	+	
nondiffuse																											
grave	+			+			+				+	+				+	+				+	+			+	+	
flat			+			+	+	+	++	+			+			+				+				+			+
sharp			+				+					+			+				+			+			+		
interr.	+	+	+	+	+	+	+	+	+	+	+	+	+	+	+	+	+	+	+	+	+	+	+	+	+	+	+
friction	+	+	+	+	+																						
slit			+	+																							
lateral				+	+	+																					
DT 1°	+	+	+	+	+														+	+	+	+	+	+			
DT 2°																			+	+	+	+	+	+			
wide glot.																											
checked																											
suction													+	+	+	+	+										
velaric																											
glottalic																											
Pos. Specs.	5	4	5	7	7	3	4	4	4	3	4	4	5	4	3	4	5	5	5	4	5	6	6	5	4	5	6

PRIMES (PSA)

	ɲ̃j	ng	f	θ	ɕ	ʈʂ	x	x	x	ƥ	s	s	š	ɕ	v	ð	ƒ	ʐ	ʐ	ʑ	ƀ	z	ʑ	ž	ƚ	m	n	ɲ̃	ŋ	l
consonantal	+	+	+	+	+	+	+	+	+	+	+	+	+	+	+	+	+	+	+	+	+	+	+	+	+	+	+	+	+	+
nasal	+																									+	+	+	+	
surd			+	+	+	+	+	+	+	+	+	+	+																	
compact	+	+				+	+	+				+				+	+	+				+			+	+				
nondiffuse							+																							
grave	+	+				+	+	+	+						+			+	+	+	+					+			+	
flat				+					+					+				+		+				+				+		
sharp	+				+									+				+		+				+				+		
interr.	+	+																												
friction			+	+	+	+	+	+	+	+	+	+	+	+	+	+	+	+	+	+	+	+	+	+						
slit			+	+			+	+						+		+	+		+	+										
lateral											+										+									+
DT 1°																														
DT 2°																														
wide glot.																														
checked																														
suction																														
velaric																														
glottalic																														
Pos. Specs.	5	4	5	4	3	4	6	6	6	4	3	4	5	4	4	3	2	3	6	5	5	3	2	3	4	3	3	2	4	2

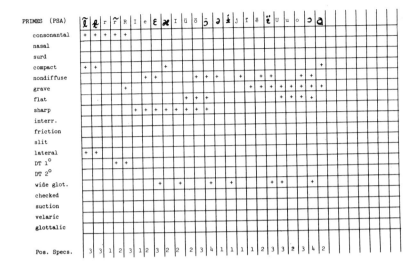

PRIMES (PSA)	ĩ	ɬ	r	r̃	R	I	e	ɛ	æ	I	ü	ŏ	ö̃	ə	ɨ	J	ɪ	ĕ	ï	U	u	o	ɔ	a
consonantal	+	+	+	+	+																			
nasal																								
surd																								
compact	+	+						+															+	
nondiffuse						+	+			+	+	+		+		+	+		+	+				
grave				+									+	+	+	+	+	+	+	+	+			
flat											+	+	+							+	+	+	+	
sharp					+	+	+	+	+	+	+	+												
interr.																								
friction																								
slit																								
lateral	+	+																						
DT 1°			+	+																				
DT 2°																								
wide glot.								+			+			+	+				+	+			+	
checked																								
suction																								
velaric																								
glottalic																								
Pos. Specs.	3	3	1	2	3	1	2	3	2	2	2	3	4	1	1	1	1	2	3	3	2	3	4	2

Appendix C
Articulatory Definitions of the Distinctive Features

For easy reference I include this set of definitions for the distinctive features I have proposed.

Contoid. Contoidal articulation is that produced by close approximation of articulator to point of articulation in the oral cavity, from the lips to the tongue back and uvula. Fricatives, occlusives, nasals, and laterals, flaps, taps, and trills articulated in this area of the vocal track are contoidal. Any other sound is non-contoidal.

Nasal. Nasal articulation is that produced when the velum is lowered sufficiently to provide a velic opening and passage of air through the nasal cavity.

Surd. This feature represents the non-phonatory state of the glottis in the speech chain. It substantiates the claim that systematic absence of sound in vocal linguistic communication can be as important as its presence.

Occlusion. Occlusive articulation indicates *total* systematic blockage of the airstream, be it egressive or ingressive. Occlusion may be contoidal, pharyngeal, or glottal.

Friction. Fricative articulation indicates an approximation of articulation which is sufficiently close to produce audible friction regardless of the phonatory state of the glottis. This is an important proviso because it distinguishes true fricatives from approximants, segments whose articulation is sufficiently close to provide audible friction only when there is no laryngeal resonance.

Slit. Slit articulation is that of fricatives which channel the air stream through a horizontal fissure. Sounds such as *f, v, Ө, đ, x,* and *g* are [+slit].

Lateral. Lateral articulation indicates that either or both sides of the tongue are raised in the production of a segment.

118

Delayed Transition 1°. Indicates that a complex segment such as [ts] or [tš] or a long segment [l:] or [a:] should be analysed as units rather than sequences of two segments.

Delayed Transition 2°. Combines with or compliments D.T. 1°. It distinguishes long complex segments č: from complex segements č by marking the former for both primary and secondary delayed transition. They compliment one another in distinguishing hypothetical segments such as *bm* and *bmb* (see 3.1.3.0–3.1.3.2).

Widened Glottis. This feature indicates that, regardless of the phonatory state of the glottis, the vocal bands are wider than normal. It accounts for tensely articulated occlusives and fricatives and for laxly articulated non-contoids as well as for murmured or aspirated occlusives.

Glottal Constriction. This feature indicates a glottis that, notwithstanding whatever other characteristics it may have, is constricted in such a way as to provide a contrast between it and a segment with less glottal constriction. It is used to indicate laryngeal creak and to distinguish strong or tense but unaspirated voiceless stops from tense aspirated voiceless stops, when necessary. It also indicates glottalized but non-glottalic sounds.

Suction. This feature indicates the systematic and significant use of ingressive air, be it velaric or glottalic.

Labial. This feature indicates significant use of the musculature to constrict, close, or round lips or to constrict pharynx in both contoidal and non-contoidal articulation.

Raised. This feature indicates articulation that involves raising the tongue higher than the upper teeth. Dental articulations, t, d, s, Ɵ, đ, are [–raised] as are pharyngeal and glotal segments.

High. This feature indicates articulation at a point higher than the alveolar ridge; prepalatal, palatal, and velar. Since uvular articulation involves the lowering of the velum to approximate the uvula to the tongue dorsum, it is [–high].

Palatal. Indicates articulation in the region of the hard palate. This articulation may be contoidal or non-contoidal.

Dorsal. This feature indicates articulation in the area of the tongue dorsum.

Velaric. This feature indicates air stream movement which is initiated by movement of the velum.

Glottalic. This feature indicates air stream movement which is initiated by laryngeal movement.

Appendix D
A Phonetic Key

Throughout this book I have tried to use phonetic symbols that are familiar to or readily interpretable by experienced phonologists and phoneticians. Owing to the different sources of my material and to the different type fonts available during the writing of this paper, my transciption has not been totally consistent. I have also had to improvise representations at times. This Appendix has been added as a means of clarifying any possible confusion that may arise in the interpretation of the phonetic characters used in this text.

Contoids -- Basic Chart

	Lab.	L–D	Dent.	Alve.	Cacu.	Pal.	Vel.	Uv.
Stop								
Vl.	p		ṱ	t	ṭ	c	k	ᴋ[1]
Vd.	b		ḓ	d	ḍ	ɟ	g	ɢ
Fricative								
Slit								
Vl.		f	θ			ç	x	
Vd.		v	ð[2]			ɟ	ɣ[3]	
–Slit								
Vl.	ɸ[4]		s̭	s	ṣ	š		X
Vd.	β[5]		z̭	z	ẓ	ž		ɢ
Affricate								
Vl.	pɸ	pf		ts		č	kx	
Vd.	bβ	bv		dz		ǰ	gɣ	

120

	Lab.	L-D	Dent.	Alve.	Cacu.	Pal.	Vel.	Uv.
Nasal								
Occl.	ɓ̃		ɗ̃	ɗ̃	ɗ̣̃	c̃	g̃	
-Occl.	m	ɱ̣	ṋ	n	ṇ	ñ[6]	ɲ[7]	
Lateral								
Vd.			ḻ	l	ḷ	l̃	ʈ	
Vl.				ɭ8				
Occ.			tl	tl	tḷ	cl		
Click				ʖ				
Vibrant								
Flap				r				
Tap				ɾ				
Trill				r̃				
Implosives	ɓ			ɗ	ʄ	ƒ	ɠ	
Clicks	q[9]			ʇ	ʗ			

---

[1]also represented as q

[2]also represented as ɣ

[3]also represented as ɤ

[4]also represented as ɸ

[5]also represented as B̲ or ʋ

[6]also represented as ɲ

[7]also represented as ŋ

[8]also represented as ḷ

[9]also represented as ƥ

Contoidal Diacritics

C^	slight raising	C:	long contoid
C'	ejection	C̄	long contoid
C?	postglottalization	ᴺC	prenasalization
?C	preglottalization	Cᴺ	postnasalization
C̦	syllabic	C̭	fronting, 1/2 step
Cʷ	labialization	Ċ	backing, 1/2 step
Cʰ	aspiration	—	friction
Cʲ	palatal timbre	C̥	devoicing
Cˠ	velar timbre	C͗	ingressive air stream
Cᵖ	pharyngeal timbre	C̈	murmur
Cᵛ	weak contoid	~	over fricatives-scraping
*C	tense contoid	Cᵍ	voiced click
C͡₁C₂	coarticulation		

Vocoids -- Basic Chart

	Front (Palatal)		Central			Back (Dorsal)	
	Rd.	-Rd.	-Rd.	Retro.	Rd.	Rd.	-Rd.
High	ü[1]	i	ɨ		ʉ	u	ï
Lax	Ü	ɪ[2]				ᴜ[6]	ï̈
Mid	ö[3]	e	ə	ɹ	ɵ	o	ë
Lax	ö̧	•	ę[4]	â		ǫ[5]	ę̈
Low	ä[7]		a				ʌ[8]

---

[1]also represented as y   [5]also represented as ɔ

[2]also represented as ɩ   [6]also represented as ɷ

[3]also represented as oe and ø   [7]also represented as æ

[4]also represented as ɛ   [8]also represented as ɑ

Voicoidal Diacritics

   ˜   nasalization   ¨   opposite articulation

   V̥   voicelessness   palatal--dorsal - Rd.

   V^V   lenition   Dorsal -- palatal +Rd.

   V: long vocoid   *   pressed vocoid (pharyngeal

   V̄   long vocoid   friction)

Glides, Pharyngeals, and Glottals

	palatal	dorsal	pharyngeal	glottal
Vd.	y[1]	w	ʕ	ɦ
Vl.			ħ	h
Occl.				ʔ

[1]also represented as j in Appendix A.

Works Consulted

Abercrombie, David. 1967. Elements of general phonetics. Chicago: Aldine.

Alarcos Llorach, Emilio. 1968. Fonología española. 4ª ed.. Madrid: Gredos.

Anderson, Stephan. 1976. Nasal consonants and the internal structure of segments. Language. 52, 326–344.

Baltaxe, Christiane A. M. 1978. Foundations of distinctive feature theory. Baltimore: University Park Press.

Barnwell, K. 1969. The noun class system in Mbembe, Journal of West African languages. 6, 51–58.

Bender, Ernest. 1967. Urdu grammar and reader. Philadelphia: University of Pennsylvania Press.

Bender, Ernest and Zelig S. Harris. 1946. The phonemes of North Carolina Cherokee. International Journal of Anthropological Linguistics. 12, 14–21.

Berry, J. 1951. The pronunciation of Ewe. Cambridge, Eng., Heffer.

Brakel, C. Arthur. 1974. Portuguese $//r \sim \tilde{r}//$, Lusitanian and Brazilian allophones, Studies in linguistics. 24, 1–15.

_____. 1977. Review of Aspectos da fonologia portuguesa. Luso-Brazilian Review. 14, 138–146.

_____. 1979. Segmental strength, hierarchies, and phonological theory. The elements: a parasession on linguistic units and levels. ed. Clyne, Hanks, and Hofbauer. Chicago: Chicago Linguistic Society.

_____. 1979a. A methodology for defining dialects and for calibrating dialect differentiation. Word. 30, 213–233.

_____. 1980. Review of Introduction to theoretical phonology, General linguistics. 20, 171–179.

_____. 1980a. Portuguese #fal+a+n$\tilde{+}$1$\tilde{+}$o# → [fá.lã^n.nu], progressive assimilation? Papers in Romance. 2, 204–210.

Campbell, Lyle. 1974. Phonological features: problems and proposals. Language. 50. 52–65.

_____. 1975. Suomen e-vartalot: lisäy vai poisto? Virittäjä. 79. 10–30.

Catford, J. C. 1977. Fundamental problems in phonetics. Bloomington: Indiana University Press.

Chomsky, Noam. 1965. Aspects of the theory of syntax. Cambridge, Massachusetts: MIT Press.

Chomsky, Noam and Morris Halle. 1968. The sound pattern of English. New York: Harper and Row.

Dixon, R. M. W. 1972. The Dyirbal language of North Queensland. Cambridge, Eng.: Cambridge University Press.

Eastman, Robert and Elizabeth Eastman. 1963. Iquito Syntax. Studies in

Peruvian Indian languages, I. Norman, Oklahoma: Summer Institute of Linguistics, 9, 145–192.

Fang-Kuei, Li. 1946. Chipewyan. Linguistic structures of native America, Viking Fund Publications in Anthropology 6, 398–423.

Foley, James. 1977. Foundations of theoretical phonology. Cambridge: Cambridge University Press.

Fudge, E. C. 1967. The nature of phonological primes. Journal of linguistics. 3, 1–36.

Geoghegan, Richard Henry. 1944. The Aleut language. Washington, D.C.: Department of Interior.

Goddard, Jean. 1967. Agarabi narratives and commentary. Pacific linguistics. 13, 1–25.

Greenberg. 1966. Linguistic universals with special reference to feature hierarchies. The Hague: Mouton.

Harms, Robert T. 1968. Introduction to phonological theory. Englewood Cliffs, N. J.: Prentic-Hall.

Harris, James W. 1969. Spanish phonology. Cambridge, Massachusetts: MIT Press.

———. 1969a. Sound change in Spanish and the theory of markedness. Language. Language. 45. 538–552.

Hasselbrink, Gustav. 1965. Alternative analysis of the phonemic system in Central south Lappish. Bloomington, Indiana: Indiana University Press.

Hill, Ken. Course packet for introductory phonology. (unpublished)

Hooley, Bruce A. 1964. A problem in Buang morphology. Pacific linguistics. 3, 35–42.

Hooper, Joan B. 1976. Introduction to natural generative phonology. New York: Academic Press.

Hughes, Earl J. and Velma J. Leeding. 1971. The phonemes of Nunggubuyu. Papers on the languages of Australian Aboriginals. 38, 72–81.

Jakobson, Roman. 1968. Child language, aphasia, and phonological universals. The Hague: Mouton.

———; Gunnar Fant; and Morris Halle. 1952. Preliminaries to Speech Analysis. Cambridge, Massachusetts: MIT Press.

———and Linda Waugh. 1979. The sound shape of language. Bloomington: Indiana University Press.

Kenstowicz, Michael and Charles Kisseberth. 1977. Topics in phonological theory. New York: Academic Press.

Kert, G. M. 1966. Saamskij jazyk, Jazyki naradov SSSR, 3, 155–171.

Kim, Chin-wu. 1967. A cimeradiographic study of Korean stops and a note on 'aspiration'. Quarterly progress report, MIT Research Laboratory of Electronics. 86, 259–271.

———. 1970. A theory of aspiration. Phonetica. 21, 107–116.

Kuipers, A. H. 1975. On symbol, distinction, and markedness. Lingua. 36. 31–46.

Ladefoged, Peter. 1964. A phonetic study of West African languages. Cambridge: Cambridge University Press.

———. 1971. Preliminaries to linguistic phonetics. Chicago: University of Chicago Press.

———. 1980 What are linguistic sounds made of? Language, 56, 485–502.

Lass, Roger. 1976. English phonology and phonological theory: synchronic and diachronic studies. Cambridge: Cambridge University Press.

Laver, J. D. M. 1969. Etsako. Twelve Nigerian languages. ed. Elisabeth Dunstan, New York, Africana, 47–55.

Leslau, Wolf. 1968. Amharic textbook. Berkeley: University of California Press.

Lisker, Leigh and Arthur S. Abrahamson. 1971. Distinctive features and laryngeal control. Language. 47, 767–785.

Lomtatidze, K. V. 1967. Abxazski jazyk. Jazyki narodov SSSR. 4, 101–122.

Maingard, L. F. 1958. Three Bushman languages, part II: the Third Bushman Language. African Studies. 17, 100–115.

Mitchell, T. F. 1962. Colloquial Arabic. London: The English Universities Press.

Mattoso Câmara, Joaquim. 1964. Dicionário de filologia e gramática. Rio de Janeiro: Ozon.

Mira Mateus, Maria Helena, 1975. Aspectos da fonologia portuguesa. Lisboa: Centro de Estudos Filológicos.

Naro, Anthony J. 1973. Estudos diacrónicos. Petrôpolis, Brasil: Vozes Ltda.

Navarro-Tomás, Tomás. 1963. Manual de pronunciación española. New York: Hafner Publishing Company.

Pagluica, William and Richard Mowrey. 1980. On certain evidence for the feature [grave]. Language. 56, 503–514.

Pike, Kenneth A. 1947. Phonemics. Ann Arbor: University of Michigan Press.

Pienaar, P. de V and A. G. Hooper. 1948. An Afrikaans-English phonetic reader. Johannesburg: Witwatersrand University Press.

Pulgram, Ernst. 1970. Syllable, word, nexus, cursus. The Hague: Mouton.

Rand, Earl. 1968. The structural phonology of Alabaman, a Muskogean language. International journal of anthropological linguistics. 34, 94–103.

Ruhlen, Meritt. 1976. The languages of the world. Language Universals project, Stanford University.

Samarin, William J. 1966. The Gbeya language. Berkeley: University of California Press.

Sheldon, Steven N. 1974. Some morphophonemic and tone perturbation rules in Mura-Pirahã. International journal of anthropological linguistics. 279–282.

Snyman, J. W. 1970. An introduction to the !Xũ (!Kung) language. Cape Town: A. A. Balkema.

Trubetzkoy, N. S. 1968. Introduction to the principles of phonological description. Trans. L. A. Muny. Ed. by H. Bluhme. The Hague, Martinus Nijhoff.

Tucker, A. N. and M. A. Bryan. 1964. Noun classification in Kalenjin: Nandi-Kipsigis. African language studies. 5, 192–247.

Tucker, A. N. and M. A. Bryan. 1966. Linguistic analyses: the non-Bantu languages of north-eastern Africa. London: Oxford University Press.

Vago, Robert. 1976. More evidence for the feature [grave]. Linguistic Inquiry. 7, 671–674.

Wang, William S-Y. 1968. Vowel features, paired variables, and the English vowel shift. Language. 44. 695–708.

Wescott, Roger W. 1965. Speech tempo and the phonemics of Bini. Journal of Anthropological Linguistics, 4, 182–190.

Wheeler, Max W. 1972. Distinctive features and natural classes in phonological theory. Journal of Linguistics. 8. 87–102.

Index